Early
Childhood
Programs

Early Childhood Programs:
Developmental Objectives and Their Use

Annie L. Butler
Indiana University

Edward Earl Gotts
Appalachia Educational Laboratory

Nancy L. Quisenberry
Southern Illinois University

Charles E. Merrill Publishing Company
A Bell & Howell Company
Columbus, Ohio

Published by
Charles E. Merrill Publishing Company
A Bell & Howell Company
Columbus, Ohio 43216

This book was set in Century Schoolbook.
The Production Editor was Deborah Worley.
The cover was designed by Will Chenoweth.

The authors acknowledge Rogers Glenn for the illustrations.

Library of Congress Catalog Card Number: 74–26178

International Standard Book Number: 0–675–08725–2

Printed in the United States of America

1 2 3 4 5 6 7 8—80 79 78 77 76 75

preface

During the last decade there has been a strong emphasis on behavioral objectives in educational programs, not only at the adult level but also as they apply to children. The area of early childhood education has been somewhat slower than other areas to respond to the need for objectives, for fear of developing programs which impose undesirable and impossible expectations on children. Yet the need for direction and understanding in curriculum planning and evaluation by early childhood teachers is no different than this need for other teachers. Early childhood programs have often been described as weak in planning and direction. In other words, they tend to take on a kind of typical form with activities generally accepted as helpful to young children, without much understanding of what is actually being accomplished.

The field of early childhood education is changing rapidly, with the development of many new programs which range in purpose from very narrowly conceived programs emphasizing cognitive development to very broadly conceived programs which seek to provide balance in the many different areas of the child's development.

Teachers find this situation quite confusing. Often they are reluctant to take a program developed by someone else for a different population and implement it in their classrooms, and with good reason. Some of these same teachers lack the background to plan their own programs. Yet seldom is adequate guidance provided for them.

In view of this situation, we feel that teachers need a basis for program planning which is based on the best information which can be put together on the development of preschool children. We feel that teachers can be helped to understand the developmental sequence of child behavior and to identify experiences to assist children at different levels of development. With this background they can progress toward planning appropriate programs with increased comprehension of what they are trying to accomplish. This book is an attempt to help teachers of children from three through five years old use broad goals and more specific developmental objectives to plan programs which are highly individualized and which respect the patterns of development of individual children as well as the general characteristics of a population of preschool children.

This book developed out of the authors' experience in a review of research on the abilities of three- through five-year-old children and the knowledge that there is a great volume of information about preschool children which has not previously been well organized into a form useful to teachers. The information in the sections on Sequence of Developmental Behavior is based on the data from our literature search combined with other pertinent data from tests and research summaries. This transition from research to a usable form is difficult to make because the pieces of data are difficult to relate to each other. In many ways it would have been easier to write a book from practical experience, and much practical experience has been woven into the sections which describe What the Teacher Does. In most books the relationship between research and application is not so directly shown, although what is written may be harmonious with the research.

Although this book is based on an extensive background of research, it is written so that it will be suitable for use in teacher education programs with the junior college or paraprofessional level student as well as the four-year college student. It is intended to be used as a supplementary text or as one of several short books which might replace a single textbook. The book also has much practical value for use by teachers in nursery schools, kindergartens, and day-care centers as a practical guide. Parents too may find it helpful.

The book is divided into four parts. Part one explains our point of view—why we need developmental objectives, some of the considerations in selecting them, and how to move into a program based on developmental objectives. Part two contains the objectives which we have developed for early childhood programs in the areas of perceptual and motor skills, helping children to think and communicate, and helping children grow socially and emotionally. Throughout this part a consistent pattern of presenting the data-based sequence of developmental behavior, the objectives we feel can be derived from these data, and a discussion of what the teacher does has been followed. The introduction to this part presents a point of view regarding the use of developmental objectives in program planning. Understanding this section is essential for use of the objectives as they are intended. Part three provides further help in planning for individual children, and part four deals with evaluation of children's progress. An example of an observational guide is included in the appendix.

contents

chapter 6

Helping Children to Develop Socially and Emotionally   120

**part three
Planning for
Individual Children**   185

chapter 7

Seeing Objectives in Terms of the Total Child   186

**part four
Evaluation**   195

chapter 8

Evaluating and Reporting Progress   196

appendix a

appendix b

appendix c

appendix d

Understanding the Why and How of Developmental Objectives

Part One includes the rationale for basing an educational program for three- through five-year-old children on developmental objectives. Researchers of child development have long provided information which is useful in the planning of educational programs; yet, this information has not always been provided in an easily usable form. Some early childhood programs have reflected little planning and little understanding of those experiences which are consistent with the abilities of children while other programs have been rigid with unrealistic expectations for children.

In Chapter One, we explain why it is important to have developmental objectives in early childhood programs. In Chapter Two, we explain how you can determine specific objectives for your program and some important factors that may affect your decisions. In Chapter Three, we explain some of the ways you can plan as you formulate a program based on developmental objectives.

An understanding of these chapters is very important if you are to use this book in the way that it is intended; i.e., to provide a flexible and personalized program for each child which has a clear direction and a sound basis for planning. Such programs should provide a maximum opportunity for children to develop during the preschool years.

chapter 1

Why We Have Objectives in Early Childhood Education

Every child has a right to the best possible environment. However, experiences and activities can be provided which contribute to his greatest potential or which tend to hinder rather than foster his growth and development. If planning an environment for children can influence their development, then educators have a responsibility to provide a good environment. Educators are aware of many activities and experiences which can enhance a child's development. Establishing objectives which define these experiences and activities will help in program planning. The objectives will also help to create an awareness of and to meet the special needs of children.

Many educators write objectives for all areas of the curriculum. They recognize the need to define what is appropriate for children at all age levels. Increasingly, educators have been expected to show what is accomplished in schools; and with this expectation has come the necessity of writing objectives that are realistic.

Early childhood educators, too, have become interested with writing objectives which are appropriate for younger children. The variety of programs developed for culturally disadvantaged children has contributed to this interest. With this interest has come the desire to plan appropriately for children with specific needs.

Why develop objectives in early childhood education? Do children do more than just play? Does very much really happen in an early childhood classroom? The reply to these questions is a resounding yes. Children learn through activities that adults see as play. Even though everyone may appear to be just playing in a carefully planned early childhood classroom, much learning is taking place. Experiences and activities must be enacted time and time again to become a part of the child. This learning process takes place most effectively through play. To insure that the right play activities are taking place, objectives are needed.

Usually, there are many pieces of equipment, materials, and games for children to play with in an early childhood classroom. Children can learn from using most of this equipment, and they will learn more if the teacher understands what the child is able to learn and what the potentiality of the equipment is. You may have heard that children's learning in early childhood classrooms should be incidental, not accidental. Without clear objectives, too often it is the accidental learning which takes place. When this happens, the teacher knows how to use equipment and experiences to keep the children happily and constructively occupied, but she does not know what can be accomplished through the experiences. Incidental learning must take place within a framework of careful planning by the teacher. The teacher must understand why equipment is good and what kinds of growth or development can be fostered in the child as a result of its use.

Early childhood educators have been remiss in developing objectives. Perhaps this is because of a fear that the objectives which they would write would be too specific. Early childhood educators know that children develop at different paces and have different interests and that not all children can reach specific objectives at the same time. Many educators feel that using objectives is contradictory to the basic principle of accommodating individual differences. However, individual differences really have implications for how objectives should be used. This knowledge indicates that the teacher should proceed with caution when writing objectives, but objectives can and should be written for young children. They should be used to provide direction and show progress but not to pressure the child toward attaining fixed standards. When identifying and trying to effectively meet the basic needs of children, our objectives must be realistic.

Children's Development Can Be Influenced

The majority of early childhood educators believe that the early years of a child's life are the most important and formative years. Researchers who study the growth and development of infants and children believe that much education takes place in the first six years of life. During this period, all of the experiences that the child has influence his development.

The Swiss psychologist, Jean Piaget, has provided a great deal of insight into a child's need for experiences. To develop in all aspects of their lives, children must interact with the objects and people in their environment. This developmental process can be strengthened if the right activities are matched with the child's needs.

Planning experiences that fit the readiness of the child and his growth is an important concept in the development of objectives for young children. Such planning can prevent, or at least lessen, problems later on in the child's life. If experiences can help a child to develop, then they should be provided.

Head Start programs have made a difference in the lives of disadvantaged children. The environmentally or socially disadvantaged child has different needs than the blind, deaf, or retarded child, although many disadvantaged children have been judged to be mentally retarded until the influence of the preschool program causes their I.Q. scores to raise. Most programs for the disadvantaged do produce at least a temporary rise in I.Q. scores as well as positive changes in language skills, nutrition and health status, and socialization.

The alternative to influencing the child's development is to let him grow and develop without guidance. This does not seem like a viable alternative in a day and age when so much knowledge is available to help teachers plan good programs. While there are still gaps in the data we have on young children, never before has so much information been available. It does not seem that we should ignore it.

Ways to Influence Children's Development

There are numerous ways in which the young child's growth and development can be influenced. A good early childhood program plans for the positive kinds of influence and attempts to avoid the negative influences.

MATERIALS AND EQUIPMENT

Providing an assortment of materials and equipment in a new or interesting way will direct the children's attention to an activity. On a playground which is void of equipment, the addition of some balls, short ropes, or a tent can positively influence the action. The addition of equipment of a more abstract nature such as a climbing apparatus enhances the child's play. Housekeeping equipment, dress-up clothes, or wheel toys can further influence the child's development.

The placement of equipment and materials at strategic places in the room will also have an influence on the children. For example, if crayons and paper or puzzles are placed on a table, children may come to the table and try them. Children are still free to bring other materials to the tables, but they are not left completely on their own if some things are already there.

The objectives which you write for each child will determine the specific equipment or materials to be used. The age of the children, their past experiences, and their stages of development all will determine what equipment and materials would be most useful.

GUIDANCE OF THE TEACHER

If the teacher carefully observes the child before interacting with him, he can foster certain desirable behaviors and forestall or prevent undesirable behaviors. To guide children and influence their behavior, teachers must realize what is appropriate behavior at a certain age or stage of development. For example, understanding that a child needs to use aggressive behavior to assert himself at the preschool stage will allow the teacher to work with this behavior and guide the child into appropriate ways of expressing his feelings.

The alert teacher guides the child's language development. He supplies vocabulary items to the child, models sentences for him, encourages him to tell stories or describe events in his life, and helps him to keep his ideas in the right sequence.

The teacher can influence the child by the way in which he directs the child in the use of equipment and materials. Holding the child's hand so he can walk the balance beam or being ready to catch the four-year-old child coming down the big slide are ways a teacher encourages new psychomotor behavior on the child's part.

EXPERIENCES

The child learns through his experiences which may be concrete (i.e., directly experienced) or vicarious, in the classroom or on a field trip, new or familiar. For the young child, concrete experiences have great meaning. He needs to feel, see, taste, and hear in order to gain an understanding of his world. This does not mean, though, that books, films, records, and other less direct experiences should be omitted. On the contrary, these materials can broaden his perspective of life. It does mean, though, that the child needs to be actively engaged in exploring his environment, and early childhood objectives should reflect an attempt to meet this need.

In addition to new experiences, children need opportunities to engage in skills and activities over and over again. This is not the same as drilling mathematical facts in the upper grades, but rather it is trying to do an activity until satisfaction is recognized within the child. A child might measure sand or water for a long period of time. He might pour the water or sand, back and forth, into two or three containers for twenty minutes. To the observer, it might look like redundant behavior; but the child may be testing a hypothesis, or he may be checking an assumption that he has made, none of which he may be able to verbalize at his young age. This repetition may be necessary to increase his understanding of a concept or to increase his skill. Making available appropriate activities for the child to "practice" is very important.

INTERACTION WITH PEERS

A child's development can also be influenced by other children with whom he comes in contact. How can a child learn to share if he has no one with whom to share? How can a child learn to enter into a group activity if he has no experiences with groups of children? How can a child learn to listen to others if no one talks to him?

The peer group provides important relationships for the young child. If a child is placed with children of his own age, he has an opportunity to learn how to get along with others. He learns what happens when another child wants the same tricycle that he wants. He learns how other children react if he yells loudly or pushes or shoves. He learns how other children react to an idea he has for building with the blocks or in the sand. These kinds of interactions influence how the child perceives himself. This perception of himself in turn influences how he acts with those around him.

INTERACTION WITH ADULTS

Interacting with adults can be an important influence on the child's development. Many children interact with only their own parents until the time that they enter school. They become used to their parents' way of interacting with them and do not know how to react to other adults.

Being with teachers and other adults in the classroom can help them learn how to adjust to differences in people. Children seem to learn very quickly what kinds of behavior an adult will accept. Parents who are permissive and find their child regulating their lives are often surprised to find their child accepting the teacher's rules or regulations in the classroom.

Just being with several unfamiliar adults can help the child learn to respond to others outside his immediate family. It can give the timid child other people with whom he can talk or play a game. It can give an insecure child someone to whom he can relate, someone who can reassure him in his efforts at school. It can give the lonely child someone who cares and shows concern for him. Finally, adults in the school environment can provide the care or other aspects of life which the child is not getting at home.

Favorable Development Requires Planning

Providing the most favorable environment for children requires thorough and careful planning by the teacher. You must consider the children, the program you want to provide for them, and the facility in which you work.

The first consideration should be given to the children. What is their background? What are their needs? Are their needs general or are there many special needs among them? What experiences can their parents provide and what experiences should the early childhood program provide?

When you have answered these questions about your children, you can consider program possibilities. What can you provide in your program that will foster the development of these children? What can you plan for them that will meet their developmental needs?

Finally, you must consider the facility in which you are working. You will want to use the space to the best advantage. Considering the space and equipment which you may already have is vital to your planning.

After examining the children's backgrounds and needs, you are ready to write objectives for your class. Now you are ready to match the needs of your group with the appropriate experiences and activities for their stage and level of development.

You will need to find the best way to meet the objectives that you write. For every learning experience a child can have, there are numerous ways to provide for it. You will consider the many ways that a child or group of children can meet a given objective.

This planning should include a continuous reassessment of the children's behaviors and needs. Objectives will change as the year progresses. The program will change as the children change. Planning must foresee this change and provide the mechanism for the program to move forward with the children.

Objectives will also change from year to year. No two groups of children are ever totally the same. There may be similarities between groups, but there will also be differences for which you must replan.

PLANNING MAKES ADULTS LOOK
AT CHILDREN'S NEEDS

Many worthwhile activities take place in classrooms without teachers ever thinking about why they occur. Writing objectives and planning from objectives make the teacher think about the learning or development that is taking place within the child. If evaluation or reassessment follows these activities, a close correspondence should develop between planned activities and the meeting of children's developmental needs.

An example of this might be explained here. Perhaps you have used the activity of letting children tear tissue paper of various colors into small pieces and paste them on construction paper. This is a common art activity in many preschool classrooms. Using paste and paper to arrange a design or simply pasting is an objective for some children, but this activity can be carried further in terms of objectives for the children. This activity can become a means for discovering how primary colors form secondary colors (e.g., pasting red tissue paper on blue tissue paper results in a purple colored space on the paper). Thus, what may be viewed only as an art activity by one teacher can become an experience in learning about mixing colors to form new ones for another teacher.

Planning for the introduction of a new piece of climbing equipment should make you think about how each child will use it. Sally will climb to the top and down again, Bill will climb to the top and call for help to get down, and Joey will not even try it. Unless you think about their possible reactions, children like Joey will perhaps never climb it during their year with you. Recognizing Joey's cautious nature would help you plan to assist him in climbing the apparatus.

WRITING OBJECTIVES HELPS TEACHERS KNOW WHAT PROGRAM EXPERIENCES WILL BE HELPFUL

You may have many ideas for working with young children. Until you actually plan for your classroom, however, you may not be sure which of your ideas are helpful for the children. Writing your objectives after studying the needs of your children and considering program implementation possibilities will provide a better match between the children and the program.

Having objectives will alert you to new ideas and experiences for the children. They will make you more aware of the learning and growth which is taking place, and they should help you to discuss individual children with their parents. Having planned specifically for these children, you will have specific facts on their development. Your understanding of young children and their individual differences will increase as you follow their progress in respect to the objectives that you have set for them.

chapter 2

Determining Early Childhood Objectives

Considering Child and Community Needs

CONSIDERING THE INDIVIDUAL CHILD

In planning for preschool children, the teacher's foremost question is, will this program fit my group of children? This question can be both helpful and confusing. It is helpful if it leads you to consider what experiences will be developmentally appropriate for the typical child. When you have decided on that average level, then you will need to plan further for the child who is not yet at the average level or who is already past the average level. This will surely be a confusing question if it leads you to believe that the typical child really exists outside your imagination. It is highly unlikely that any child will be at the average level of his age group in all areas of development. If you should find that some child does fit that description, you can be almost certain that he will not remain there long; he will probably rush ahead of the average level in some areas and fall behind in others.

After you determine what the typical child is like for a particular developmental characteristic, you should also ask what the children who are least typical on this characteristic are like. When you know what the typical and the least typical child are like for a particular developmental characteristic, you can determine which children are the most developmentally advanced or delayed in this regard. To accomplish your goal of advancing each child in this area, you will need to provide experiences which fit the needs of the most developmentally advanced and the most developmentally delayed children. Let us call this the *range* of experiences needed. By helping each child to advance past his starting point, you will meet your developmental objective in any particular area.

You may wonder, what is the value of knowing about the typical child if you must plan for each child? There are two values. First, the chances are great that some of the experiences which you plan for the typical child will hold some interest for the more advanced child, and even if they are presently too challenging for the developmentally delayed child, over the course of the year he may begin to work on these experiences. This means that you will get much use out of those learning opportunities which fit the average child. A second and closely related point is that it is helpful to have some idea of how many children are likely to desire and benefit from particular learning opportunities. If you know something in advance about these expected numbers, you can arrange additional space for the high demand opportunities while you provide less space for those activities which will interest or challenge only one or two children. This portioning of work space and materials will change as the class needs change. Thus, even if the typical child exists only in the teacher's imagination, thinking about him can help with classroom planning.

CONSIDERING THE COMMUNITY

Some early childhood programs have a well-defined philosophy and firmly established procedures for working with children. They may have little occasion to consider the wider community so long as it provides a steady flow of children whose parents wish to have them in the program. For these programs, the community is limited to the parents of those children who are enrolled. Such programs often remain unchanged year after year because their philosophy suggests that they are already doing all that they should do for their children.

Their communications with the community may be confined to explaining to parents what is happening in the program and how the child is progressing. Montessorian programs display many of these features.

On the other hand, some programs respond to particular community needs. For example, a program may be established especially for children of working mothers, low income families, or full-time students. Another program may focus upon family development and offer broad opportunities for parent involvement and growth in child-care skills. The connection between community needs and program emphasis may be so intimate that the program is funded by the community or some unit of government. Head Start serves as a prime example of a community-needs oriented program.

The majority of programs probably fall somewhere between the two examples of community responsiveness. The majority are probably responsive to community wishes to some extent but not fully. The directions for a program will generally be based on a viewpoint that considers what early childhood education should be and how to meet the developmental needs of children. So long as the community needs do not conflict with this viewpoint, a program can be responsive to the community. Sometimes, however, forces within a community may endorse regimentation, indoctrination, or other professionally unsupportable goals. When this is the case, the early childhood professional should resist these unwholesome community forces. The relation of your program to your community will affect how you select objectives.

How Staff, Facilities, and Budget Affect Objectives

When determining objectives, several features of your program need to be balanced off against each other until the best combination is reached. Considerations which are related to staff, facilities, and budget may affect how many and which objectives can be selected.

STAFF

If you are starting an entirely new program, how can you recruit and hire, within your budget, the necessary staff? In this case, you have a very wide set of choices because you can look for a staff which has special skills in working with the objectives that you have chosen. Usually, however, you will be starting your program with part of your prior staff; so you will have a special set of questions to ask about their preparation to move into the new program.

First, you will want to consider the skills and experiences of your staff. Are they able to work with the kind of objectives that you are planning to use? For example, suppose you have decided to work on objectives in the fine motor area. Staff skills and experiences which might be helpful for these objectives would be skills in observing and recognizing children's fine motor behavior, knowledge of manipulative experiences which are interesting and challenging to the age level, beliefs in the importance of fine motor development, ability to judge a suitable match between children's fine motor skill levels and materials, and so forth. A brief survey of staff skills and experiences will be most meaningful if you write it out and use it to examine program plans.

It is not necessary, however, that the staff members possess all of the desired skills so long as they are willing to learn and try new things. This kind of staff flexibility will allow you to move into new directions more easily than any other characteristic.

Staff attitudes toward children and their development will affect your decisions about setting objectives. If staff members easily accept new objectives, they will be willing to learn new skills. Because staff attitudes will affect your decisions, you may find it desirable to involve your staff from the very beginning in the selection of new objectives. This course of action will prove wise, even if it does not entirely fit your personal viewpoint of involving staff in this manner.

FACILITIES

Gross motor objectives can be handled on a modified basis with an indoor facility, but outdoor space with appropriate equipment is necessary if you are to have a strong program of these objectives. Napping facilities which can be isolated from active, bright, noisy areas are essential for a full-day program and objectives which are related to it. Kitchen facilities are also required for full-day programs whereas a pantry and refrigerator may suffice for part-day programs.

If you plan to have parents observe without disrupting activities, you should have an inconspicuous location for them to observe their children. A one-way mirror/window is ideal. You may be able to have it installed between your classroom area and an office or storage space which is large enough and well ventilated for visitors. Observational facilities are also useful when you wish for one of your regular consultants to observe something in particular. Finally, this permits you to cooperate in the training of early childhood personnel who need to observe selectivity before they become directly involved with children.

Ample storage is a must for nearly every program. Your staff needs to be able to accumulate materials and store them in an easily accessible area. The more imaginative your program and the broader your set of objectives, the more essential will be your storage needs. Individual lockers for wraps and other storage by the children belong in every early childhood center; without these, you cannot easily teach children how to be responsible for their own things and leave alone the things belonging to others.

Facilities for water play, sand play, and other kinds of sensory experience activities belong in centers that stress fine motor objectives. These kinds of activities prepare the child for forms of fine motor construction (e.g., building sand castles) which involve imagination.

As you are probably aware, working parents will sometimes bring a child who is on the verge of illness or who is recovering to your center. Sometimes a sudden illness will appear after the child has arrived. These emergencies call for a comfortable isolation area with

While older preschoolers build intricate sand tunnels, younger preschoolers fill and dump trays of sand.

a window connection to the classroom. In such an area, the sick child can rest and play quietly without being overly stimulated and without infecting the others. The visual contact afforded by the window keeps the child from becoming lonesome or feeling deserted and permits the teacher to see if the child requires special attention.

Various other features of a facility are optional for some programs. A bus or carry-all vehicle keeps you from being bound to the center. A chapel, stage, isolated play therapy room, or space for consultants to work or meet with parents may seem like luxuries, but if any of them is vital to your program, you should plan for it.

BUDGET

We have considered staff and facilities independently. Actually, they are closely related in your planning, and both are affected by budget. Your aim is to use the strengths of both your staff and facilities to the maximum benefit possible within your budget. In this way, you will be able to help children develop in relation to your objectives; but if you spread your resources too thin by trying to do more than is possible, your program is likely to be less helpful to children because it will be less effective. These choices require making difficult decisions; but it should be reassuring to know that by choosing carefully, you will, in the long run, accomplish more with the children and their families.

We will look first at some budgeting considerations and then at some tips for stretching the budget. The budget in most programs is assigned primarily to personnel salaries and wages. Staffing patterns affect these costs. For example, if you use an all professional staff, your budget will be higher than if you also use aides. On the other hand, if you use aides, then your professionals must have skills in the areas of supervision and in-service development of aides. Budgeting requires you to consider the relative costs of each total pattern of staffing. It is generally desirable to have a sufficient amount which is budgeted for part-time help or substitutes to stand in when regular staff members are ill. Otherwise, the children may receive too little attention and supervision at times. Transportation costs, food services, utilities and building overhead should be budgeted. Provision is made for specialist services. Finally, part of your budget should provide for buying and replacing classroom equipment and materials. This last budget item should include contingency funds for unanticipated needs in this area or for unusual opportunities that may arise to make purchases at favorable prices.

Costs in some of the preceding areas can be reduced or eliminated by learning how to refer children to other agencies for services which you cannot afford to provide, by borrowing or making things from scrap materials, and by appealing to your advisory or parent board or other community groups for help in obtaining certain items which are needed. Careful planning of job descriptions can permit you to acquire one or two utility persons who can double in more than one capacity, thus increasing your staff's flexibility without increasing overall cost. One sign of an effective program director is his creativity in obtaining those items that the budget does not provide for directly.

Fitting Objectives to Your Program's Important Goals

HOW OBJECTIVES RELATE TO GOALS

In considering how objectives relate to goals, it will be helpful for you to know how we use these terms. In the educational field, goals and objectives are often used interchangeably to mean "purposes which have been set or established." However, in current usage, a distinction has begun to be evident between the two words. Goals are generally stated purposes; objectives are specifically stated purposes. Because goals are broader than objectives, each goal will imply two or more objectives. For many years, the standard practice of educators was to produce statements of goals. More recently, objective statements have been adopted widely as the standard. This changing practice has been confusing to many educators. They have wondered if the emphasis on objectives is an effort to do away with goals.

Another term which is used widely today is behavioral objectives. This has a more specific and limited meaning than objectives. Behavioral objectives are planned observable events (i.e., outcomes). These three terms can be arranged from general to specific as follows:

General - Specific
Goals   Objectives   Behavioral
                                                        Objectives

During the recent shift toward the adoption of behavioral objectives, people seem to have taken sides for either these or goals. Without a sense of broad goals, behavioral objectives become isolated, overly narrow purposes which, on the positive side, are observable. Without specific behavioral objectives, broad goals are like good intentions which do not lead to action. Therefore, goals and behavioral objectives should be complementary to each other.

Goals can be broad developmental objectives. Because they relate to the fundamental processes of society and child development, the early childhood educator feels justified in defending them as worthy of emphasis. Because goals give us this large perspective needed for program planning, the early childhood educator will want to begin with them. Around each broad goal, a number of specific objectives can be identified. Behavioral objectives represent particular parts or strands of any broader developmental goal. The word "strands" emphasizes the unity of goals and objectives—these strands are woven together into a unitary fabric of development. This is a fundamental relationship, because objectives, if they are based on developmental sequences as we have defined them, are also developmental in the sense that their natural, observable sequence has been established by careful research. We can imagine artificial, man-made behavioral objectives which are not fundamental because they are neither based in children's development nor discovered through research. We reject these artificial behavioral objectives because it is scientifically impossible to know whether they will really contribute to any of the broad goals which strive toward helping children to develop.

Since goals refer to the broadest developmental purposes, objectives to purposes of a more specific developmental nature, and behavioral objectives to the particular outcomes, our discussion hereafter almost always treats goals and objectives and seldom refers to behavioral objectives. Finally, we have used the term "developmental objectives" to refer to the level already discussed as objectives (not behavioral objectives). Sometimes we have used the term "broad developmental objectives" to refer to goals.

SELECTING OBJECTIVES AND EXPERIENCES
TO MATCH GOALS

Now we can move from the preceding general discussion to specific examples. Suppose that one of your broad goals is to help children develop positive peer relationships. A number of developmental strands or developmental objectives would appear to contribute to this broad goal. We know that children are more able to enter into peer relationships when they are less dependent upon adults. Thus, a developmental objective to achieve greater independence from adults would be a possible part of your plan. As children's imaginations develop, they progress beyond an interest in things to an interest in how human relationships work and are organized. Progress in this area moves them into cooperative forms of play and, as a result, increasing peer relationships. We also know that the child's ability to think of what he wants to say and to express his ideas verbally increases his success in peer relationships. Finally, if the child has the gross motor ability to participate in the activities that his peers are doing, his peer relationships will be improved.

The preceding example illustrates how complicated a goal may be in the sense that many separate developmental attainments contribute to it. We can be sure that the goals of developing positive peer relationships will be advanced by working on objectives in the areas of thinking and communicating, growing socially and emotionally, and developing perceptual and motor skills. Furthermore, the illustration is not complete because there are more factors which relate to positive peer relationships. For example, the development of cooperation and positive social behavior also contribute.

Since several behavioral objectives potentially contribute to the development of each goal, you will probably want to work on all of these at once but not equally. Some children will already have sufficient levels of development in some of these behavioral areas but will need special help in other areas. Experiences need to be made available in each developing behavior area at a level which is appropriate to the child's current development. Help is offered in the selection of experiences to match each objective in Chapters Four through Six.

Striving for a Comprehensive Program in Areas of Development

Apart from the kinds of goals already discussed, an overriding concern of many early childhood educators is the goal of furthering the development of the whole child. Attention should be given to helping children develop perceptual and motor skills, develop cognitive skills, and grow socially and emotionally. You can examine your program to see how much it gives attention to each of the three areas.

Balanced attention to the three areas would be desirable for most normally developing children. However, when children have special needs, more attention may have to be given to particular areas. In Chapters Seven and Eight, more attention will be given to planning for children with special needs. The main point to be made here is that you will need to strive for that balance which will best serve the child's individual development.

chapter 3

Moving into a Program Based on Developmental Objectives

In order to implement new objectives, you will have to look at all aspects of the program to see which ones are harmonious with your objectives and which ones need to be changed. Moving into a new program can increase enthusiasm for your job because you will probably feel that you are doing something which is right for your school and your children. As you see the responses of the children, you can feel the excitement of their learning and their success. To most teachers this is a very rewarding experience.

Moving into a new program can also cause feelings of uncertainty. Since you have not tried the ideas before, you will not always know whether they are going to work. Sometimes it will be difficult to try new approaches because as an experienced teacher, it will be much easier to use the skills you already possess rather than to learn new ones.

Developmental objectives will give new direction to your program. For one thing, you will no longer wonder what you are trying to teach children; you will have definite ideas. Developmental objectives provide direction without holding you to one set of specific experiences. You will also have the opportunity to create ways of working which appeal to different children in your class.

Someone from outside your school may be able to help you over some of the rough spots. You may obtain this help by inviting someone to look at your program and talk with you about it. You may also get some help by going to visit other teachers who are working on a similar program. You may learn how to make and use equipment and materials through workshops. It is difficult to predict exactly what kind of help you will need until you get started.

Objectives May Require Changes in Your Classroom and Outdoor Areas

Part of the planning to begin the use of developmental objectives includes a decision regarding the materials and setting you will need. For each objective, plan experiences that you can give the children to help them learn the required skills. Think about materials and equipment you already have, and consider using some equipment in a different way.

CHANGES IN MATERIALS AND EQUIPMENT

Children in your classroom will have different needs in relation to each objective. If your objective concerns eye-hand coordination and the children are putting puzzles together to accomplish it, you will need some simple puzzles for the children who have never worked puzzles before, for younger children, and for any child who has difficulty putting puzzles together. If you want older children to be interested in the activity, provide puzzles that are a little more difficult to assemble. Children will enjoy working a puzzle several times after they learn to do it well, but they will soon lose interest in it. You will need a new puzzle or activity if you want them to continue to practice with puzzles.

For each developmental objective, list the materials that you will need. First, think about the basic equipment that you probably have like blocks, books, art materials, sand, and carpentry tools. Then think of materials that can be improvised from waste materials that are already on hand or can be obtained from the parents or others. After matching the material and equipment in the classroom to the objectives and experiences, you will need to see where you can get additional things. If you have material that does not fit any of your objectives, trade it with a teacher of older or younger children for something she cannot use that is usable with your children.

After examining your materials, you may find that there are several objectives that can be initiated almost immediately and that there are others that can best be started later. At this time, set your priorities for the equipment which you will need to purchase. Most schools will not be able to buy everything that is needed at one time. Yet, equipment must be available so that children who have different abilities can progress toward the objective, and sufficient amounts of the equipment will be needed so that several children can participate in an activity at the same time. If possible, materials and equipment should be adaptable for use in reaching more than one objective. For example, a child can develop creativity with some of the same materials that he uses to develop fine motor coordination. He can develop language abilities with some of the same materials that he uses to develop social behaviors.

CHANGES IN ARRANGEMENT

Working toward developmental objectives requires that some specific principles of room arrangement be followed. Changes will be needed if these principles have not been used previously.

Certain centers of interest will be determined by the objectives. Plan these centers so that the children will assume as much responsibility as possible for getting out and putting away materials. Low, open shelves enable children to get toys out and put them away when they have finished. Equipment on shelves should be located consistently in the same place so that the child knows the place for equipment that he uses. Whenever possible, arrange a space for using the equipment near its storage area; this prevents getting out and putting away problems.

Sometimes a trial and error process will have to be used to determine what to do about noisy and quiet activities. The basic principle of arrangement is that noisy activities should be placed close together and quiet activities should be placed together. Another principle that helps to avoid conflicts is to arrange shelving and screens in such a way that traffic is guided away from the main area where children play with blocks, art materials, and other things that can be thrown or knocked over.

Probably there should be centers for blocks, art, looking at books and listening to records, science, math, quiet games, homemaking, music, and carpentry. There might also be a cooking area, or you might rearrange one of the other areas for this purpose.

Often there are features of the room which will determine where different areas should be located. Before you change your room arrangement, look around and find out where the electrical outlets and heating vents are located. If the floor is partly carpeted, the carpet will help to absorb part of the noise of the noisy activities, but cleanup after messy activities will be easier if they are placed on tile or other surfaces. Art materials and most other messy play materials should be placed near a sink; this makes cleanup easier and keeps the children from putting messy hands on chairs, toys, and other children. The location of windows and doors should influence the placement of activities. For example, windows should not be blocked so that children can stand in front of them and look out at the snow or the birds.

CHANGES IN THE STRUCTURE OF THE PROGRAM

The structure of your program should enable individual children to progress toward developmental objectives at their own rate. Thus, you must plan the structure of your program to encourage different children to engage in different activities. Plan to limit the use of total group activities, such as listening to stories, which require about the same responses from all of the children.

You will need to provide some large blocks of time. Within these time blocks, the children gain from having the opportunity to explore an ever-changing array of experiences. During this time, let children remain in one interest area or with one experience as long as you can keep them interested. During one hour, some children may stay with one activity for almost the entire time while other children who have not learned to sustain interest may move from one activity to another several times. These will be self-chosen activities although the choices will be controlled somewhat by what is made available, what is new to the classroom, and what has been there for several days.

Experiment with the amount of time during the school day that is given to a choice activity. Some programs are devoting a large majority of the school day to a block of time in which the children pace themselves. Other programs find that helping children to participate in group activities is important and start with short group discussion times combined with the reading or telling of a story or singing songs. As long as the group activity is kept short and the children's interest is maintained, this kind of activity may be within the focus on developmental objectives. However, anytime you have a range of student differences, keep much of the time available for individual selection of activities or individual instruction.

CHANGES IN EQUIPMENT OF THE OUTDOOR AREA

The quality of the outdoor areas varies widely from school to school. Some schools have a carefully planned and well-equipped outdoor area. Some schools have no playground of their own, or if they do, the playground consists of a wide open space with little or no equipment of the proper kind and size for preschool children. Of course, the kind of playground that you have will determine the kind of changes that you will need to make. If you already have a well-planned outdoor area, it may need little change.

View the outdoor play area as an expansion of your classroom. The equipment, then, will need to provide for activities which can be conducted in the outdoor area where there is less need for restraint of physical activity or noise level. Such equipment will encourage children to climb, stretch, jump, and test their physical skills. The more versatile the equipment is, the better. If the same piece of equipment that is used for climbing can also be used for the "hide-out" and the "ship," it will receive much greater use. If ladders, walking boards, and large crates can be arranged in many different ways, the children will spend more time testing their skills on them than if they are usable in only one way. Versatility of the equipment along with a quantity of equipment which is great enough to encourage participation by several children without interference with the activities of others will help the children learn to get along with each other.

CHANGES IN THE ARRANGEMENT OF THE OUTDOOR AREA

If you want to use climbing apparatus for a dramatic play such as the "fire station," you will need to have a hard riding surface that comes near the climber so that children can get their "fire engines" close to the station. If you want to successfully grow flowers and vegetables in the garden plot, it will need to be located in a remote area of the playground and protected from stray tricycles and wagons that are carelessly ridden. If you want your hard surface to be of maximum use, it must extend from the playground's exit to the classroom in order to be reached without getting into water or mud on days when the grass and soil are wet. If you want your equipment to be put to many uses, you must have some pieces which are portable and can be used in various ways as well as moved from one area of the playground to another.

While there should be some large open areas for running, rolling kegs, or playing games, there should also be some areas in which sociability is encouraged. A large sandbox with room for several children to play at one time and with some short wide boards for sitting on or for dumping sand or a table set up for children to work with clay will make it possible for children to balance the more active play activities with ones that are quieter and more restful.

CHANGES IN THE USE OF THE OUTDOOR AREA

Some outdoor areas have been used simply as a place where children can run, climb, or ride tricycles to let off steam. The teachers in such a situation usually do not take any initiative for suggesting activities to the children. They simply supervise the activities to see that they are safe and that one child does not interfere with the play of another child. There is nothing wrong with this kind of activity. Additional activities can be offered on a choice basis. Tables for art activities and games can be moved outside, and you can sit under a tree and read or tell a story on a warm day.

However, if you view the outdoor area as an extension of the classroom, you need to look carefully at your developmental objectives and determine which ones can be met in the outdoor area. We usually think of the gross motor skills first in relation to this area, but too often we rely on the same activities day after day. Change the activity in accordance with the skills of the children so that the activity is difficult enough to be a challenge to the children but not so difficult that they cannot be successful. Cognitive as well as affective objectives can be met in the outdoor area.

Objectives May Require Changes in the Skills Needed by Your Staff

Any kind of program change calls for the development of new skills by the teachers who are responsible for putting the program into action. If the program which is being changed has previously been a laissez-faire program with a maximum of freedom for the children and little direction from the teacher, the teachers will need to learn ways of stimulating children's activity and learning in the specified directions without any negative effect on the children's ability to choose their own activities. If the direction of the change is toward giving the children a greater degree of freedom, an entirely different set of skills will need to be learned by the teachers. Some of the changes will be in the organization of the classroom; others will be in the skills of working with children.

CHANGES IN CLASSROOM ORGANIZATION SKILLS

Organize the classroom so that the children will have maximum time to engage in the activities which lead to your objectives. For example, if you think that it is important for children to do as many things as possible for themselves, organize your day so that children have time to take off and put on their own clothes, so that they will be able to get out and put away their own toys and equipment, and so that they do not have to ask for help every time they are confronted with a problem. Since the development of vocabulary is dependent upon the new experiences that children have which introduce them to new words in a meaningful context, you will arrange the necessary experiences and provide opportunities for vocabulary development. If the children's time is to be used well, the transition period from one activity to another should be minimized.

For a classroom using developmental objectives, more planning is needed and more activities must be provided than if all the children do the same thing at the same time. The teacher organizes herself, her staff, and her planning but provides a high degree of freedom for children to organize themselves. The situation has the appearance of being free. The children are doing what they want to do within a wide range of choices. What the observer does not see is the planning that the teacher does to provide classroom materials and activities that will both interest the children and provide the experiences that they need to accomplish the developmental objectives that are right for them at the time.

CHANGES IN THE SKILLS OF WORKING WITH CHILDREN

You can easily be misled when observing a teacher who is doing a good job of implementing developmental objectives. The job looks so easy, and the teacher may appear not to be doing very much. Much of the activity may seem to function without very much intervention from him, or when he is involved with small groups and individuals, the interaction is very informal. The appearance of such a classroom is very different from the classroom in which the teacher gives directions, begins and terminates the activities, and generally dominates the situation.

Planning.   The first kind of change you may need to make is in the way you do your planning. If a developmental objective is stated specifically, the problem you face in planning is how to move the child from where he currently is toward the accomplishment of the objective. You have to make a judgment about the process that the child will follow in accomplishing the objective and about where he is in this process. Self-chosen activities have the advantage here because the child is able to set his own goals and is not as likely to encounter standards that he cannot reach.

The factors of interest and ability are the constant concern of your planning. You do not have to wait for children to show interest before you plan an activity. Children have not had the opportunity to develop an interest in all of the things that might be of interest to them so you can do much to broaden their interests. The key guideline is that if you cannot interest the children in the activity, forget it and move on to something else. There are many ways to accomplish the same objective. Everything you try will not work. Some things will work for one or two children but not for very many. The quicker you recognize this, the more able you will be to try a variety or activities, thereby increasing your chances of reaching all of the children.

Planning also involves developing new materials and getting previously developed materials ready. Before school and after school time should be used for the getting-ready process. Many good experiences are ruined because the teacher did not follow through on this step of assembling the materials so that the teaching time would not have to be interrupted to find the forgotten item or to mix the paint that was too muddy looking to use.

Setting Up the Activity.   Instead of setting up the same activity for all the children or relying upon the equipment to carry the program, new activities must be set up each day; and these activities should be attractive so that they will interest the children. Activities may be set up in the interest area to which they relate. If this is done regularly, the children will look carefully around the room to see what is new and of interest to them. This will help reduce the tendency of some children to return to the same interest area day after day to do the same activity over and over again. While all children will have favorite activities, it is important that you help them to become aware of other centers.

As new activities are set up, try to anticipate the number of children that will be attracted to them at one time. While it is nice if you can provide a child with the activity that he wants at the exact time that he wants it, this cannot always be accomplished, especially if the new activity is particularly attractive and only a few children can work at one time. Decisions regarding how many and for how long may become necessary if not many children are attracted to the same activity at the same time.

CHANGES IN LEADERSHIP SKILLS BY THE DIRECTOR

Just as the teacher assumes a strong leadership role in encouraging behavior which is consistent with the goals of the program, the director also assumes such a role in relation to the teacher. For the director who has been accustomed to making most of the decisions, this is a change, but it is also a change for the director who has allowed teachers almost complete freedom in making decisions. The basis for decision making is the set of developmental objectives that has been developed, and the director provides leadership in helping the teachers to meet the objectives.

The crucial issue in the directors leadership is not whether the director knows how to implement the objectives. It is much more than this. The director must have confidence in the ability of the staff to implement the objectives and must be able to get their best ideas of how the job can be done. The process that applies to the work of the director with the teachers is the same as that used by teachers in their work with children. It recognizes, supports, and encourages the maximum use of their potential in directions which are consistent with the developmental objectives. Teachers must be encouraged to try new ideas and helped in as many ways as possible to see that their efforts will be successful. When new ideas are tried, occasional mistakes will be made. There must be enough rapport within the staff that individual teachers feel free to discuss what has happened and seek solutions to problems. Much of the support that is offered by the director is a moral support which communicates to the teacher that the director believes in him. Some other kinds of support which the director may provide are availability of materials, easing the way with parents and other teachers, and provision of extra staff or volunteers for activities which call for additional help in the classroom.

An ability to provide strong leadership in planning is one of the prime prerequisites for the director. Some leadership consists merely of making the mechanical arrangements; however, it is more important for the director to see that the planning is effective and has meaning to the people involved. They can see that what takes place in the planning meetings improves the program, and they are honestly stimulated by the planning that takes place. Meetings do not necessarily accomplish anything, but meetings which deal with significant problems and involve important decisions can make a big difference.

The director also assumes some of the decision-making responsibilities that are rightfully part of his job. This is often forgotten. There are times when decisions must be made quickly and decisively. There are times when the teachers' behavior is entirely out of line with the objectives decided upon by the staff. Whenever this problem occurs, the director must deal with it. For most directors this is an unpleasant task, and they will hesitate to handle it for fear of creating worse problems than already exist. If the situation has not been allowed to become serious, the chances of working out the problem are improved. If the rapport within the staff is good, one incident is not likely to change it appreciably. The positive and supportive action of the director must be strongly felt, and the negative and corrective action must be used sparingly. The leadership role of the director must be respected, and the limits must be clearly understood.

Changes in the Involvement of Parents

If you are to achieve the maximum value from a program based on developmental objectives, do as much as possible to provide for consistency between the expectations of the child at home and at school. Teachers become very familiar with the behavior of the child at school, but the parents know the child long before he enters school. Parents have their own expectations for the child which are based on their family values and the levels of achievement that other family members have attained or not attained. When the parents have had a choice, they may have selected a particular school because of their understanding of the program and its appropriateness for their children. If the program is changed too much, the same parents might not be interested in the school.

Parents should be involved from the very beginning in discussions of changes in program. They are interested in improving the program as much as you are. Parents can be involved in advisory boards. You want to create the feeling that this is "our" school and we all care what happens here rather than a feeling that the school belongs just to the children and the staff. If there is no parent organization, you may wish to create one in order to provide a way to select certain parents to represent the group. Consider, too, that parents who may be very interested in the school and the changes that are made may not feel that they have very much to contribute to this kind of planning and may need considerable encouragement while others may need essentially no encouragement. These attitudes may have little to do with the potential contribution of the parent. Consider, also, that fathers are parents and may bring a different point of view to the discussions. When a parent organization, complete with committees, already exists, the process of involving parents in an additional activity is an easy step; but if you must begin with a situation in which parents have not been involved, you will need to proceed more slowly and involve parents gradually. If parents are very familiar with a program, as they often are in a cooperative nursery school where participation in the classroom is a regular activity, you can expect a very informed kind of input; but if a parent has never visited the classroom, this may be the place to start.

Parents are more appropriately involved in the decisions regarding the selection of goals than in the selection of specific objectives and their implementation. Many parents will be quite clear regarding what they want for their children. Discussions which develop may be very enlightening to you and may open areas of discussion that the professional staff may not have considered. You may agree or disagree with the parents. Very likely, you will do both, and the discussions will modify your opinions as you search for consensus. Try to make sure that everyone has the opportunity to express his opinion although every opinion will not appear in the final statement.

Since only a few parents can be involved in the actual process of deciding on the objectives, provide a means by which all parents can be kept informed. Newsletters can be one means of communication, but reports by the participants at meetings where all parents can have an opportunity to exchange ideas will keep the discussion more open and provide information about the parents' acceptance of the changes that you are planning.

Use of Community Resources

From your experience in working with the educational program, you will have some idea about how it is regarded by the community. A public school is usually regarded as a community activity; but many private schools and day-care centers are regarded as private enterprises, and their relationship to the total community is felt only by those families who are participants in the program. Frequently, neither the school nor the community makes an active attempt to explore ways they can be helpful to each other. The involvement of the community is consistent with the involvement of the parents and can contribute to the program of the school.

As you focus on developmental objectives, consider ways that you can relate the program of the school to the life and activities of the community. Consider the community to be the total learning environment in which the activities of the school can occur. This will include ways that the program can be moved out into the community through field trips to enlarge the experiences of the children. It will also include thinking of ways that the life and happenings of the community can be used in planning the school program. To do this, a great deal of knowledge about the community is needed, especially a knowledge of the people in the community who have special interests or hobbies that may be related to the school program. Parents will be helpful in providing some of this information, but you will also want to involve the staff in finding some of these things as this will help to develop an enthusiasm for using the resources.

Keep a continuous file of community activities and resource people that might be available to the school as up-to-date as possible. In this file, be sure to include an appraisal of how young children are received and whether there is someone available who can meet them on their level. Some people are so afraid that very young children will be hurt or will interfere with the regular activity that they do not give them a chance to find out what they could learn. Others simply do not know how to talk to children or how to get the children to respond. When you take children into the community, you want to be sure that the experience is going to be worth the time and effort. You want to know ahead of time what the learning possibilities are so that planning with the children will focus on finding out the right information.

You will have to take the major initiative in bringing the program of the school closer to the activities of the community, particularly if it is a proprietary or cooperative school. Becoming involved with other schools of similar purpose is one step you can take. Common problems and concerns often become the basis for a working relationship that develops between professional people and parents of different programs. Parents often provide the link to the larger community.

In a nonpublic school, one of the most difficult contacts to make is with the public school or schools in which the children will later be enrolled. We would hope that the kindergarten or first-grade teacher would be interested in learning about the program that some of the children might have had in nursery school and would also be interested in the experiences that particular children have had as well as their accomplishments in the program. We would also hope that mutual planning between the schools would help to reduce the discontinuities in learning that often occur when children move from one program to another. You may be able to do little more than propose that discussions be held. Visits might be arranged to the schools if nothing more is possible. Past history indicates that the problems to be worked out are difficult and largely dependent on the interest of the teacher who will have the children the next year as well as the way he perceives his job.

Striving for a Comprehensive Program in Available and Needed Services

The school may not want to immediately provide a volume of specialty services. Yet, if you plan for a comprehensive program, you will need to locate all community resources and prepare a list of referral sources. As you help families locate these services, you can be sure that as much as possible is being done to meet the children's needs.

NUTRITION

Both undernutrition and overnutrition are problems which are seen in preschool age children. A specialist in child nutrition uses an interview to complete a survey of family eating patterns, may study a twenty-four hour food intake of the child, evaluates subcultural preferences for particular foods, and in very young or motor handicapped older preschoolers examines feeding, chewing, and swallowing habits. Children who are underweight, overweight, or who show a nutritional deficiency should have a thorough nutritional checkup. Your center's food services can follow the nutritionist's recommendations, which should also be shared with the children's families. Some enforcement responsibility may be given to the early childhood educator at lunch or snack times.

MEDICAL

Most centers require a health clearance before admitting a child into the program. This report alerts the staff to special health needs of the child, as, for example, the need for restricted activity or protection. Attentive educators will occasionally notice a new condition which should be referred to the child's family physician. Usually, telling parents about this will do the job. A problem is posed whenever the health of other children is threatened by a child whose condition can be passed along to them; for example, lice, ringworm, impetigo, and some eye inflammations, as well as respiratory infections. None of these diseases are usually covered by public health laws as are tuberculosis and venereal diseases, but often the local public health office can offer advice and perhaps treatment.

Parents should be required to complete an emergency information form which expresses their exact wishes about how any medical emergencies shall be handled. You may find it necessary, whenever the families you serve do not have regular medical contacts, to have access to a pediatrician who will treat your emergencies. In a comprehensive program, you may become aware of limiting conditions that have not been reported for the child before. For these cases, you will need the advice of a pediatrician about which kind of specialist the parents should be told is needed.

DENTAL

Dental screening and instruction in dental hygiene have become a standard feature of some preschool centers. Routine screening can often be arranged for groups of children through public-minded dentists, whenever parents cannot afford private services. This is an area which should not be neglected, since the foundations of dental health are being developed during the preschool years.

MOTOR DEVELOPMENT

Typically, a normal motor development program will be available through the early childhood center. If the child, however, has an unusual pattern of motor behavior that suggests that an injury has occurred or that the child has been affected by some disease, special services will often be needed. An orthopedic physician or osteopath may recommend these special services, or in some places, they are available from a physical therapist or an occupational therapist. In less severe conditions, physical education or recreation specialists may be prepared to offer services. Examinations for motor problems are sometimes provided by all the persons previously mentioned. Generally, physical therapists who specialize in children will be the most competent in gross motor evaluation, and child occupational therapists will be the most competent in fine motor and aspects of sensory evaluation. A well-planned therapy program may prevent the development of a serious disability, particularly if therapy is started early in the preschool period.

PSYCHOLOGICAL

At the preschool age level, developmental evaluation, emotional or mental evaluation, and some forms of therapy may be desired. Pediatric psychologists, child clinical psychologists, some school psychologists, and some practicing developmental psychologists provide these services. If the psychologist whom you locate performs developmental evaluations, this person will be helpful not only for making decisions about exceptional children but also for consulting with your staff about developmental objectives and goals.

SPEECH AND LANGUAGE

Persons who are qualified in this area deal with problems of hearing, expressive and receptive language, and the basic skills which contribute to language and speech development. While preschool age children are often not yet mature enough to work in speech therapy, various things can be done to help language development in children who are language delayed, unless the delay is primarily the result of mental retardation. A speech and language specialist might provide valuable consultation to your staff regarding these objectives.

SOCIAL SERVICES

Families experiencing stress or disorganization often require temporary help. Social services for families are provided by private and public agencies. Some social agencies are operated by religious groups (e.g., Lutheran, Catholic, Jewish, Volunteers of America, Salvation Army). The Community Action Programs have also provided services in this area in recent years. Traditionally, these services have been available through the local family service agency or the county welfare department. The early childhood program center may be in a unique position to recognize family needs and to suggest these referrals. If the problem is of a crisis or mental health nature, the community mental health clinic or child guidance clinic may be the referral choice. Regular social work consultation to the early childhood center can provide preventative as well as treatment purposes.

Moving into a New Program

Some teachers and parents feel a lot more comfortable with the status quo than with a new program. Some are interested in moving quickly into something that is new and, to them, more challenging. In most any school, you will find both kinds of people. The balance of the kinds of people on the staff and in the parent group will determine whether you move into a new program by trying out a few objectives at a time or whether you make an abrupt change from one year to the next.

TRYING OUT OBJECTIVES A FEW AT A TIME

The most gradual method of moving into a new program based on developmental objectives is to select one or two of the most important or needed objectives and put them into effect, perhaps even before all of the work has been completed in developing the total program. This puts the parents and the staff in a position of engaging in dual planning—planning on the one hand which is related to developing the objectives and planning on the other hand which is related to the implementation of the objectives. This approach has the advantage of getting something new into effect while the people who are doing the planning can implement it. This process is worthy of consideration if the time can be found to hold workshops and discussions about how the program is going to be different and how the difference is to be evaluated.

Both teachers and parents may be more secure with trying out a few objectives at a time because it does not mean an abrupt change. They can feel secure about the things they already know how to do if too many changes are not made at one time. The disadvantage, however, is that not very much may change; and it will be easy to slip into old ways without even being aware of it.

PLANNING AN ALL NEW PROGRAM

If teachers and parents can find the time during the summer to design the new program, the changes could be made when the school opens in the fall. The advantage to this approach would be that much of the planning time could be separated from the implementation time, and the program could be evaluated during the school year. The staff could feel better prepared to move into the program, and parents, if they have been participating all along, would also know what kind of program the children would be entering. Much of the new equipment could be acquired before school opens, and major changes could be made in the room arrangement and outdoor area if necessary.

An all new program might also be planned in two or three year phases with the school identifying how many changes are planned for each year. More important than how the plan is implemented would be the adequacy of the planning to implement it.

INTERPRETING CHANGES TO PARENTS AND
THE COMMUNITY

Even if there has been parent and community involvement, more publicity must be given to the changes so that there is a constant awareness of them. One reason for this is that although people from the community may have been involved, many people in the community may not have been involved. Some of these people will be interested; and beyond that, they may also be affected by the plans. Materials may be prepared for the parents. Newspaper publicity may be helpful to the community. If there are local newssheets where no local newspaper is published, this may be one of the ways to provide information. Holding open house for the community may also help to bring about some understanding. Many ways should be used, and some evaluation of the effectivenss of the publicity should be made. Suggestions probably will come from members of the community as a result of these attempts. Criticisms are almost inevitable. These community responses should be given a fair hearing, but they should also be kept in the perspective of whether they are consistent with the goals. Every suggestion or criticism will not be appropriate. Those who are responsible for the final plans will have to make a decision regarding the feasibility of all suggestions.

Objectives for Early Childhood Programs

Part Two is designed for direct use in program planning. These three chapters are directed toward the teacher who is deciding what to do with the children in his classroom, toward the student who is learning to plan experiences for children, or toward the parent who wants to know what kinds of experiences to provide for his child. Chapter Four includes the physical aspects of development such as growth and maturation, gross motor development, fine motor development, and speech. Chapter Five includes the cognitive or intellectual aspects of development that enable children to think and communicate; this chapter includes perception, memory, concept development, language, mediation, and problem solving. Chapter Six includes the social and emotional aspects of development such as personality factors, motivation, social perceptions, and social behavior.

These chapters include the specific information about development which we need to assess the child's abilities and to find out some of the abilities he should develop next. A consistent pattern is followed in each of these chapters. First, we have identified areas which research and test data have indicated are appropriate for goals and for which there are enough data to support development of guidelines. Second, from these data we have identified specific objectives for preschool years. Then we have tried to show what the teacher can do to help a child progress toward these objectives.

In each chapter the developmental guidelines have been grouped into five levels of behaviors which are commonly seen at about the same time in individual children. The viewpoint which makes these guidelines useful to the teacher is not associated to age level but to developmental level, so references to age are left out. The levels should not be confused with stages. The entirety of early childhood can be divided into either one or two stages, depending upon one's viewpoint. Because levels are not stages, you should expect some children to show a clearly observable mixture of behaviors from the levels that are immediately next to each other. The levels are clearly sequential, probably overlapping for children who are in transition.

Two concerns are associated with these guidelines. First, children should be in a program that meets their developmental needs. If you observe a child who is being considered for your program, there should be a good match between the child's developmental level and what your program can offer. Since our focus is on the years three through five (up to the sixth birthday), we would be concerned if a child who functions at a level lower than level I were included in a program that cannot meet his developmental needs. On the other hand, by the time a child has advanced beyond level V, he can most likely benefit from a first-grade experience. Level V thus fits into the kindergarten or readiness level.

Second, because the levels within an area are sequential, we do not expect to see mixes across levels that are not next to each other. For example, within gross motor development, we would not expect a child who functions within level III to show level I gross motor behaviors. If he does show this kind of discontinuous mix, the child needs a thorough developmental evaluation (see suggestions in Chapter Three). You should not be as concerned if a child with a fine motor level IV pattern shows a gross motor level II pattern; however, you should attempt to determine if and why he is having problems in the school situation. A thorough understanding, based on professional evaluation, can lead you to recommend special services for the child and can inform you of the experiences in your program which are needed most by this child.

Most objectives as they are stated apply to level IV and V behaviors. With children who are behaving at the lower levels, there are intermediate objectives which you must set based on the child's performance. Working toward an objective means moving a child through the sequence of behaviors leading toward the objective. The basic guide is to plan experiences through which the child can take the next step in the sequence. In no way do we intend to imply that all children of the same age or in a class will be at the same place in the sequence at the same time. Neither do we expect any two children to reach the objective by the same process. Children use experiences differently. Plan for this kind of flexibility in your program.

The developmental levels information in Chapters Four–Six is based on several research sources. These sources have been carefully sifted and compared with each other to determine those aspects of development which are based on findings rather than on expert opinion. If you are interested in examining some of these research sources, you will find them listed in Appendix A. They include the results of our own literature search of over 1,000 studies of preschool children's development.[1] We have blended our ideas with these other major sources on child development, developmental testing and screening, children's language, children's personality, and some widely-accepted standardized tests.

Since our sources provided considerably more data in the cognitive and social-emotional domains than in the perceptual and motor domains, we were able to develop more objectives in those two domains. This does not mean that we advocate the emphasis of one domain over the other. Rather, our goal was to identify those objectives which could be supported by the data. It was the data which were unbalanced. An educational program should provide a balance among the three domains.

---

[1] Annie L. Butler, Edward Earl Gotts, and Nancy L. Quisenberry, *Literature Search and Development of an Evaluation System in Early Childhood Education* (ERIC #'s ED 059780–059784, 1971). (Available through the Early Childhood ERIC, Urbana, Illinois)

chapter 4

Helping Children to Develop Perceptual and Motor Skills

Gross motor behaviors refer to the child's control and use of the large muscles of his body, particularly the legs, arms, and neck, although the muscles of the shoulders, back, chest, abdomen, and buttocks play an important part in the child's ability to control his extremities. Gross motor behaviors have been grouped into five levels. These levels are constructed parallel to the same numbered levels for fine motor and roughly parallel to those for speech and for growth and maturation. Some children are more advanced in one aspect of psychomotor behavior than others because of temperament, motor development characteristics, interests, and other influences. Some children show a clearly observable mixture of gross motor behaviors from levels that are next to each other. A child who shows both level I and level II gross motor behaviors is one who is developing level II behaviors. Level I behaviors should be considered as minimal for participation in a program for three year olds. Children who have not yet reached this level need a program designed for infants and toddlers or should be cared for in their homes. A few three year olds will be in level I, many in level II or a mix of I and II, and many in level III or a mix of II and III. You are unlikely to find a three year old at level IV, although your most advanced three year olds may occasionally show some level IV behaviors mixed with a majority of level III behaviors.

Fine motor behaviors refer to the child's control and use of the small muscles of his body. This includes hands, wrists, and eyes, and especially how they work together. *Speech* refers to the motor and perceptual aspects of the child's speaking. It includes his ability to hear and to produce the speech sounds which are used in his environment. Other aspects of the child's language are discussed in Chapter Five. *Growth and maturation* refers to the physical development of the child in height, weight, and proportions and to the influence of health and nutrition upon these. These three areas together with gross motor behaviors make up the important parts of how children develop motor and perceptual skills during early childhood. Sometimes this area of behavior is collectively called the *psychomotor* area. Two psychomotor senses have not been mentioned. Touch along with vision is included here under fine motor behaviors. The child's sense of his body and position in space is called *kinesthesia*. This is discussed under gross motor behaviors. You will recognize those parts of the discussion by noticing that *touch* is referred to as sensory aspects of fine motor and that *kinesthesia* is simply referred to as balance or as body control.

We have divided self-help skills into those which reflect social development, which appear in Chapter Six, and those which reflect motor development, which appear in this chapter. If you are working with handicapped children and find it important to concentrate on self-help, you will recognize from the Vineland Social Maturity Scale or from the Preschool Attainment Record that all of those behaviors are included in either Chapter Six or this chapter. We think that it is more useful to think of these behaviors in terms of areas and levels of developmental behavior rather than to treat them as isolated items of behavior around which to build objectives.

At level I and level II, the child shows a large amount of functional play. *Functional play* describes a total pattern involving simple muscular activities; repetition of actions and manipulations, imitating oneself; trying new actions, imitating them, and repeating them; speaking, repeating what one has said, and imitating speech. Functional play allows the child to practice and learn his physical capabilities and to explore and experience his immediate environment.

Functional play is gradually replaced with *constructive play.* Through this type of play, the child learns the various forms of play materials, moves from functional activity to activity which results in a creation, sustains play longer and develops an ability to concentrate, and sketches a theme around which to organize his play. Development from functional to constructive play marks a shift from manipulation to formation, from handling and experiencing to building. The child who achieves play goals that he sets for himself is able, in part, to achieve play goals set by others. Level III shows a mixture of these two play types, with functional play weakening a bit. By levels IV and V, constructive play is more prominent. This movement through the levels is seen in the amount of time which younger preschool children devote to gross motor activity and the greater amount of time which older preschool children spend in fine motor activity. *Symbolic* or *dramatic play,* which includes *social play,* begins to appear at level IV and is quite strong at level V. Since its major significance is for children's social and emotional development and somewhat for their thinking and communication, it is discussed in Chapters Five and Six.

Finally, you should be aware of some cautions. Much of what has been said about levels will not apply to the behaviors of motor handicapped children, although these developmental descriptions will still be useful for letting us know what the child is doing or can do. Among children who have no motor handicap, individual differences are obvious. Evidence suggests that black children are more advanced in gross motor activities that require physical coordination than white children, throughout the age range of early childhood. All of these cautions should make you aware of the importance of observing each child carefully and planning for each child individually.

Gross Motor—Sequence of Developmental Behavior

Level I.   When a child enters an early childhood program, we expect him to run without falling or tripping often. He leans forward with his shoulders hunched while running. Arms are held away from the body and to the rear of the body for balance. The child uses stairs with the help of a handrail or by running his hand along the wall for balance. He still places both feet on each step before proceeding. Children's skills for going upstairs are predictably ahead of the comparable skills for going downstairs. He easily squats with knees bent to play; but when reaching for something from the standing position, he is likely to remain stiff legged, bending over from the waist toward the ground.

All in all, his assurance in the upright position is reflected not only in running and on stairs but in other things that he does or will try upon request. He will, for example, try to stand balanced on a walking board and will eventually attempt a step or two, but without alternating the foot which is placed forward; he will jump from a bottom stair step and will eventually jump from the second step, clearing the bottom step; and he will walk backward, although unsteadily. He can be shown how to stand on tiptoe; a little later he will take one or two steps on tiptoe. These acts together show that he is not likely to lose his balance and does not always need to have both feet under him. He can, for example, step forward and kick a large ball at this developmental level.

He can also do things with his arms, without having to pay as much attention as formerly to keeping his balance. Examples of this include his ability to pull a toy after him while in motion, to toss a small ball without tumbling, or to slip off a coat or dress. The same assurance of balance and position in space which permits the child to tread stairs or try the walking board may get him into difficulty when he climbs onto furniture which may not provide dependable support.

The child's sense of rhythm is developing at this level. He may begin to use such equipment as a rocking chair, rocking boat, or rocking horse.

Level II. At this level, the child may climb more, pulling himself up and over obstacles, or he may climb to a high spot for the view or to reach something which he desires. A simple climbing apparatus attracts and holds the child's attention at this level.

The two sides of the child's body are becoming dependable as independent sources of balance and stability. The child now stands on one foot or even balances momentarily, hops on one foot two or more times, steps alternately left and right along a walking board, and alternately places the left foot and then the right foot while going upstairs, placing only one foot per step. Soon the child will alternate his feet like this when going downstairs.

The child's legs are also increasing in strength. Now he can, with his feet together, jump forward; or he can jump from the second step of a stairway, clearing a distance of one or two feet. After the child starts jumping, he will soon be able to clear two to three feet on a

*With the aid and encouragement of their teacher, singing the
"Bear Went over the Mountain," these children practice their
climbing skills.*

level jump. About this time, he can also jump over a string or other
obstacle, soon advancing from a jump of only one or two inches to
possibly one of six to ten inches.

The combination of improved balance and leg strength enables
him to run forward in a straight line rather than weaving, to avoid
obvious obstacles, to walk along a straight line heel-to-toe, and to
push or pull large objects while playing. From lying flat on his back,
he now stands by pulling himself forward to a sitting position, putting his legs under him, and rising to the standing position. While
standing, the child can now slip on a coat or dress without help. He
stands straighter than before, with shoulders back more.

Level III.   The child's gradually independent balance on his left and
right sides becomes surer with increased muscle size and strength.
The child can walk on tiptoe for some distance, pedal a tricycle, kick
a large ball with ease, balance on one foot for several seconds, and
eventually hop about on one foot. He squats comfortably when playing on the ground or floor.

His increased agility permits him to dart past obstacles or to turn
corners while in motion and to avoid accidents when he is dragging

or pushing large objects such as a wagon or a box full of toys. Motion, such as that on a swing which requires joint rhythmical use of arms and legs, is now manageable. Listening to rhythmical music and making simple movements in rhythm will also be observed.

Increased arm strength and control are observable. The child can steer his tricycle or grip a swing. He catches a ball that is bounced to him. He climbs with confidence. Whereas he previously rolled or threw a ball underhand, he now throws it overhand. At first, the wrist is stiff when throwing; that is, the arm is raised and bent at the elbow, leading to the use of the shoulder and elbow in the throw.

Level IV. The child can balance on either foot for ten or more seconds. He hops about on either foot, skips on one foot, and even skips to music. He can use musical rhythm or other forms of external regulation to take part in group activities, such as a group circle dance. He is surer of himself on a tricycle, or when climbing, running, and jumping. He may thus try more risky things. The distance jump of two or three feet can now be done at a run. He can walk backwards, alternately placing the toe of one foot behind the heel of the other. Rather than picking up objects stiff legged, he bends his knees slightly, extending them outward as he leans over at the waist. He can hold a ball against his body with the pressure of his arm, leaving his hand free for other activities. The child can dress himself, except for tying his shoes.

Level V. The child's rhythmical movement increases over that of the last level. Feet alternate in skipping, and the child can play rhythm games which require concentration, such as dancing. His rhythm shows up in his ability to skip rope. The child uses his total body well enough in imitation to play follow-the-leader. He can run and prance about lightfootedly without falling while playing games. He hops repeatedly on either foot, showing increased motor control. At this level, the child will try to skate, sled, and steer a wagon, although accidents are to be expected from time to time.

Arm and hand strength are increased. This increased strength is seen in the child's grip, the force with which he hurls a ball, and his ability to climb a ladder. More challenging climbing equipment will attract his attention.

Not only has his gross motor control and agility greatly increased but his ability to suppress or inhibit movement is also better than before. He can remain balanced on one foot on a small spot without weaving, shifting around, or hopping to stay up. He shows motor inhibition in his ability to sit for longer periods of time without becoming restless. Gross muscle control is closely related to the rating of greater muscle tone, although this will not be true for some children who have particular motor handicaps (these children may have excessive muscle tone). Some children who are otherwise showing good gross motor control will, nevertheless, be low in the area of motor inhibition. Temperament is probably responsible for much of this. Children who lack motor caution will disregard their physical safety and are less ready for school than the child who exercises caution.

With these accomplishments, the child has advanced enough in the gross motor area to enter formal schooling. Some educators have given much attention to handedness, dominance, and laterality, as if these are clearly related to readiness. Actually, there is little solid evidence to support the current interpretations of handedness and mixed dominance as they are said to relate to motor development. We do know that most children show a preference for using one hand over the other by about the age of two years, but the preference does not become stable until around six years of age. Joint usage of both sides (ambidexterity) is more common before six years of age than many professionals realize. No attempts should be made, therefore, to influence a shift of the child's handedness except on the special professional advice of an unquestioned authority. We also know that when the child learns the left-right distinction (not the same thing as handedness), he first learns it in relation to his own body and later understands it in terms of the left and right sides of objects or persons. The labels *left* and *right* are of course only names arbitrarily assigned to directions and will only be learned if they are taught.

GROSS MOTOR OBJECTIVES FOR PRESCHOOL-AGED CHILDREN

1. To engage in a variety of activities which require balance and total body control.
2. To engage in a variety of activities which require rhythmic movement.
3. To dress oneself with the exception of tying and difficult fasteners.
4. To climb large climbing equipment such as slides, jungle gyms, fire poles, abstract climbers, etc.
5. To ride and guide wheel toys such as tricycles and wagons.

WHAT THE TEACHER DOES

Specific behaviors which are given in the different levels of behavior are helpful in diagnosing where a child is in his development. You must establish the level at which the child is functioning before you can know what experiences will be appropriate for him to have. You should provide the equipment and guidance which will permit the child to practice the skills he has already acquired and to learn new skills.

A preschool child should be active during a good portion of the school day. Opportunities to walk, run, jump, climb, and pull oneself around on equipment should be provided so that the child engages in a variety of these activities each day. Equipment such as walking boards, climbers, swings, and large blocks should be in accordance with the abilities of the children. For the youngest children, boards should be low and wide, space between the rungs on climbers should be less than half the height of the child, and swings should have belted seats that are low enough to enable the child to put his feet firmly on the ground. As children become older and more skilled, the equipment needs to be more challenging to accommodate their developing skills.

You can encourage the desired activity by the arrangement of the equipment, lending a helping hand to an unsteady or uneasy child and seeing that equipment is used safely. Usually, you can safely allow children to choose whatever activity they want to engage in after having done a reasonable amount of stage-setting, but sometimes you may informally initiate an activity such as pretending to be galloping horses where you and the children may gallop around the playground, holding out a hand to some children who are less likely to participate. Beyond stimulating an activity, you may find guidance is needed with safety, taking turns, and property rights rather than with the actual skills the child is practicing. Children who are well guided during their early motor experiences progress much during the preschool years, and while the teacher must always be aware of safety, the children can become quite proficient at controlling both their bodies and the social situations created by their active play.

You can provide rhythmic experiences through the use of rocking boats, swings, or with musical instruments and records which will stimulate the child's spontaneous responses. You may use a drum to beat out different rhythms for the children, or you may play the drum or piano to the pace of the children's rhythm. You may find it more satisfactory to use an instrument that will enable you to enter into the activity or to play a record which leaves you free to move around with the children. Hopping, skipping, running on tiptoes, dancing, and various kinds of imitative activities are helpful as well as the more creative movements generated by the child's spontaneous responses to music or created out of his mood and inclination of the moment. With the youngest children, only one or two of the children may engage in the activity while several children who are approaching level V may engage in an activity. You should encourage the child's spontaneous activity, but redirect behavior that is silly or out-of-bounds. It is a good idea to establish some general procedures when group activities are provided such as "come back to the piano and sit down when the music stops." Otherwise, beginning a new activity requires bringing the children back to the group.

Some children have had little experience with dressing themselves before they come to school. This is less likely to be true of five-year-old children than of three-year-old children, but it does happen. You will not only have to be concerned with what the child can do for himself but also be aware of what he is willing to do for himself. The school setting is conducive to learning to put on one's clothes if this seems to be expected. You must be near to straighten out a sweater, see that the right shoe is on the right foot, or straighten out a pair of inside out sleeves or pants legs. The dressing activity often stops when the child encounters a task he cannot do without help. You can get children to do a lot more if you do the one little part that they have not yet mastered. Getting the zippers started, tying caps, and tying shoes usually are jobs for the preschool teacher. Reminders of the next activity or attention to some specific activity that the child enjoys may help him to move along. You have to check that all caps and mittens are on and that boots are put on if needed. Sometimes you need to talk to parents of children who dress them too warmly or not warmly enough.

Climbing equipment tends to be very popular with preschool children; therefore, an important part of the supervision is arranging the play area so there are several pieces of climbing apparatus which can be used independently. It helps if you have several pieces of equipment that can be arranged in different ways and at different heights. Walking boards, ladders, a portable slide, and several bridges or sawhorses can be arranged differently to provide constant variety. Children need help in learning techniques for climbing safely, for going down the slide safely, and for checking the steadiness of equipment that has been rearranged. You have to watch for crowding on the apparatus which might lead to a push, for children who tend to stop at the top of the slide, for children who get off a teeter-totter without warning, and for many other safety factors. For older children who have a good mastery of climbing, a variety of accessories should be provided which will enable them to combine their climbing activity with dramatic play. For the older child, the abstract climbers are sometimes popular because they can become anything within the child's imagination.

For younger children, toys are needed which encourage them to push and pull things or other children around. Activities such as pushing another child in a doll carriage, pushing around a wheelbarrow full of sand, and sitting on top of a wooden truck are popular with the youngest children while those that are a little older become fascinated with the tricycle and the wagon. Scooters tend to have limited appeal, and some pedal-operated cars are more difficult to operate. Teachers need to give the child assistance in learning to ride and steer a toy; and once the techniques of using the equipment have been mastered, it usually becomes necessary to give some guidance in using it safely. As with the climbing apparatus, guidance in actual use of the equipment becomes less necessary as the children learn to use it competently and begin to utilize it in their dramatic play. At this later stage, guidance often helps to settle disputes over who is to use the equipment or who may take part in the play.

Fine Motor—Sequence of Developmental Behavior

Recently, much professional concern has been directed to children who have fine motor development problems. Some of these problems result from defective vision. Visual defects are often present in early childhood. This calls for vision screening tests and referrals for correction. Perceptual-motor training programs have become available. Evidence suggests that such programs increase children's learning readiness but do not overcome basic visual-motor deficiencies. Immature and unsettled children do not greatly benefit from such training. Children from low income families often appear to be about one year behind children from middle income families in this area by the time they reach kindergarten age.

The material for each developmental level of fine motor behavior is organized in the following approximate sequence: finger grasp and hand control, drawing, imitative drawing; hand-eye coordination; visual acuity and form recognition; color discrimination; wrist control; manipulation as action and as sensory activity; constructive activity; and left-right coordination or midline skills.

Level I.   At this level, the child pinches with the forefinger and thumb exactly opposing each other, thus permitting exact grasping movements. The child can pick up pins, pills, and other tiny objects, can turn the pages of a book, and begins to cut with safety scissors.

His grasping behavior makes it possible for him to hold a crayon or thick pencil, although he may still grasp it with his fist to control its length. He makes a spontaneous scribble and will imitate a vertical stroke and a horizontal stroke or strokes. This ability also shows his level of hand-eye coordination, as does the picking up of tiny objects.

Hand-eye coordination is further revealed by his skill at taking things apart or putting them back together. For example, he places a wheel back where it belongs on a toy car or properly holds together the parts of a broken doll. He uses a fork and drinks from a glass without assistance. He can rapidly place round pegs into round holes and square pegs into square holes of a pegboard.

The child's visual acuity and form recognition skills are considerably advanced beyond infancy. However, his eye movements are irregular, sweeping, and nonsystematic. He recognizes objects or miniatures of objects and pictures of common objects. He places a square, circle, and triangle in a form board. It is evident from a comparison of these visual perceptual behaviors with his drawing ability that recognition is well ahead of the motor ability to reproduce what is seen. This is true at all preschool age levels.

The child's manipulative ability is increased by his greater use of wrist motion; he can, for example, turn a door knob. Much of his manipulation is not, however, intended to accomplish some result but is instead an end in itself. That is, he manipulates repetitively in the process of experiencing sensations and is mastering the performance of particular motor actions. Actions of this type include rolling, pounding, pulling, and squeezing clay or other pliable materials; scrubbing paper with a paint brush with no apparent concern for the placement of colors; filling containers with water, sand, or dirt and then emptying them, only to repeat the action; and splashing water and kneading or spreading sand. For these reasons, he prefers action toys like cars and boats.

Although he engages in few constructive activities spontaneously, he may with encouragement or in imitation build a tower of six blocks or an imaginary train of cubes. He will also tightly pack blocks into a box in which they will fit only if they are properly arranged in rows.

His left-right coordination at or across the center or his body has advanced to the point that he can unwrap a small candy or a piece of gum, make an egg beater operate, and imitate the folding of paper.

Level II. At this level, the child uses his pincer much like he did at level I, but he is more likely to use his fingers rather than his whole hand to grip a pencil or crayon. He carries breakable objects without accidents. Control over the fingers permits him to wiggle his thumb while the rest of his hand is fisted.

With pencil or paint brush he experiments with vertical and horizontal lines, dots, and circular motions. Although he may start out by trying to produce a particular form, he quickly shifts into the action of painting or drawing for its own sake. If he is asked to make a more complex figure, such as a cross, he will often make the number of strokes required, thereby showing that he knows visually what is required, but both of his strokes are likely to be horizontal or vertical without any lines crossing. He can copy a vertical line and a horizontal line, which he could only imitate earlier. Copying is more difficult for children than imitating, so it consistently comes later for a comparable form. He can roughly imitate the letters *V* and *H* because they involve a combination of strokes which he has mastered or is near to mastering. He can imitate a circle but probably cannot copy one.

Hand-eye coordination is a bit faster and surer than before but no other developments appear. About the same thing can be said for form recognition. He is faster in his performance but is not yet dealing with many new geometric forms. Eye movements are about the same as at level I.

He sometimes gets carried away with the sensory aspects of his play. He may, in fact, paint the table, easel, floor, his own hands, or other children in the excitement of the action. If he paints on paper for a long period of time, little variety will be seen from picture to picture; he will repeatedly complete a very similar drawing. Finger painting interests him more for the manipulation and sensation than for the form or effect produced. Crayons also interest him. Color discrimination is apparent from his ability to sort objects by color. He makes pies and muffins or cupcakes from sand or dirt, patting and smoothing the contents of the baking utensil.

Considerable advance is evident in the area of construction. His towers may rise to seven or eight blocks in height. When he lines up blocks and pushes them like a train, he will add a block for a smoke stack in imitation. He will place two blocks a small distance apart and put a third block across them to form a bridge, if you demonstrate this. If he fails to accomplish this, he will form a three-block pyramid in the same manner. Some symmetry begins to appear in his spontaneous building with blocks.

He takes apart more complicated things than formerly and tries to reassemble them but may be unable to do so. He unbuttons his clothing in front but cannot yet rebutton it. He is able to dry his own hands. All of these are behaviors which require the hands to meet at or cross the midline of the body.

Level III.   At this level, the child is likely to use his fingers to grip a crayon or pencil; however, if he is trying to place a short stick into a hole in an object held in his other hand, he may still use a full fist grip on the stick. By this level, many children can make scissors do what they want them to do—except for following a desired outline. The thumb can be wiggled on a fisted hand on either the left or right side. The thumb can touch at least two of the fingers on the same hand.

Horizontal and vertical strokes are imitated with a greater resemblance of the product to the original model. The child attempts to make more capital letters, especially those involving horizontal and vertical strokes. Paintings done at the easel are a little more recognizable as pictures. He copies a circle and can draw the head of a person. He is likely to include one other detail on the head—probably the eyes which you may not recognize as such, but he will assure you of what the detail is. He will imitate the horizontal and vertical strokes of a cross with intersection.

Hand-eye coordination is no longer dependent on binocular viewing. With one eye covered, the child can pick up pins and other tiny objects. He can string beads onto a cord or shoestring. He can place tiny pellets into a small-mouthed bottle. The child can discriminate more forms and can visualize which line of a series is longer. His eye movements are only slightly more systematic. He easily sorts black and white objects into piles or containers, and his color discrimination is better for sorting.

Sensory and repetitive aspects of his manipulation are less prominent. He can use a hammer or mallet to drive nails or pegs. Constructive activity is advancing. The child's tower is now nine blocks high. He can build a three-block bridge from a model, so he is less dependent on the imitation of a model's action.

The stringing of beads, which calls for left-right coordination, is developing further. Now the child begins to button a coat or dress. The child washes his hands by himself but would not yet be described as being neat at the sink.

Level IV. Further hand control is evident in the child's ability to touch his thumb to each finger on the same hand.

The major fine motor developments at this level occur in hand-eye coordination, particularly in drawing or copying. The child's ability to match or discriminate between more difficult forms increases, and there are further signs of hand-eye coordination. For example, he begins catching a ball in midair. His visual movements over the surface of an unfamiliar object are becoming more rapid and systematic, and they are less likely to drift away from what he is inspecting. When he draws a person, the face is now more complete, probably containing in addition to the head's outline the eyes, mouth, and nose. A little later two or three additional details will be added to the human drawing. When an incomplete man is presented, the child adds three or more completing features. He can copy capital letters involving circular forms. He will print the first letter of his first name and will try to print simple words. The child does free drawings with pencil or crayon. He draws a simple house. He copies a cross, square, star, left diagonal, right diagonal, and puts the two diagonals into an X-shaped cross by copying.

Sensory aspects of fine motor activity are much less prominent and have virtually disappeared in some children. Finger exploration is likely to be used in conjunction with visual searching to examine something new—so touch is being used to gain information rather than in a repetitive sensory action. The child will attempt more challenging forms of constructive play with Lego blocks or other available materials. A tower of ordinary finger blocks is now ten or more blocks high. He will build a six-block pyramid in three steps following a demonstration. He will imitate a door or gateway so that a car or other object can pass through.

Left-right coordination progress can be observed in the child's tendency to hold his paper steady with one hand while writing or drawing with the other. He can fold a paper three times following a demonstration.

Level V. The child's hand control is further developed. He can now spread butter on bread. He picks up and drops small pellets into a container very rapidly.

The child copies a triangle, a rectangle with center diagonals, a square and circle which touch at the lower right corner of the square (lower left may be better if the child is using his left hand), three intersecting lines resembling an asterisk (*), and a cross with arrow points at the ends of each arm of the cross. He can trace around a diamond shape. He prints his first name in large and irregular letters. He frequently reverses letters, especially *S*. He prints the numbers one through five. His free drawings are outlines without shading. When he colors outline drawings, he stays within the lines. Later, he colors right up to the lines, but still no shading is present. He draws a house with door, windows, roof, and chimney. When he draws a person, it is now recognizable by head, body, legs, arms, and facial features. Ten or more total details are present at this level. He adds seven parts to an incomplete man. Cutting with scissors becomes, at about this level, a form of tracing, with the child following the outline of a simple figure while cutting.

More complex forms are correctly matched or placed in a form board. Puzzles have become a favorite activity for some children. The child's visual precision allows him to lace his own shoes and to catch a ball five inches in diameter. His visual searching of new objects is more rapid and systematic. His eyes seem to estimate the distance between the parts of a figure and move as if to trace a figure's outline.

Before he reaches the degree of mastery described above, the child rough cuts (i.e., approximates the outline) with scissors and follows up by pasting. Thus, within this level, cutting shifts from being a type of constructive play to being an aspect of copying realistic shapes by tracing with the scissors along the outline. At this level, the child can make a three-step pyramid of six blocks from a model; he no longer requires actions to be imitated. Tinker Toys, Lincoln Logs, and other commercially available construction sets become interesting to the child.

The child's left-right coordination permits him to fold paper in a complicated manner to match a particular form. For example, the child can fold a square paper into a triangle, and he can then fold the triangle into a smaller triangle in imitation of a model. He buttons more difficult buttons, such as smaller ones. With a shoelace, he ties a simple knot around a pencil in imitation of a model. Toward the end of this level, the child will tie his shoes in a loose bow.

When his fine motor skills have reached this level, he is essentially ready for the first grade within this area.

FINE MOTOR OBJECTIVES FOR
PRESCHOOL-AGED CHILDREN

1.   To develop the hand control which is essential for writing, drawing, and handling eating utensils.

2.   To develop the eye-hand coordination which is essential for using construction toys and moderately difficult puzzles and form boards.

3.   To control scissors when roughly cutting (i.e., when cutting approximately) along the outline of a simple figure or design which the child has drawn.

4.   To acquire the coordination needed for lacing, paper folding, buttoning, or loose tying.

WHAT THE TEACHER DOES

Many of the same pieces of equipment and many of the same materials are used at each level of development of the fine motor skills. The children use the materials and equipment in ways that are appropriate for their own stage of development. You should provide duplications of materials across levels. The children will show you through their choices which materials are appropriate for them and which are not.

Provide many items such as beads, pegs, buttons, shells, seeds (beans, corn, etc.), and other small items which will give the child practice in grasping small objects. With younger children or with children who have never tried these activities, you may need to show them what to do. You will probably have to put a few pegs in the peg boards or string a few beads. Show the children how to sort different kinds of beads or seeds, and then stay with them to see how they handle the objects. Suggest that they paste buttons, seeds, and other small objects on collages.

At all levels, children will enjoy using crayons, pencils, felt-tipped pens, chalk, and paint brushes. Provide many opportunities for the children to explore these media and to develop their skill in handling these tools for writing, drawing, and painting. You may see a need to demonstrate the use of these materials, but you should not expect more from a child than he is developmentally able to do. It is important for the young child to have the opportunity to express his ideas using these tools in his own way. *Your ideas should not be forced on him.* Your expectations of how to represent a tree, house, or cow should not be forced upon the child. Many times children will want to use these media without making anything specific. This should be encouraged.

The use of eating and cooking utensils also provides opportunities for the child to develop his fine motor skills. You will have to use snack time or juice time, if your program does not include lunch, in order to give the children experiences with these utensils. Let them spread butter, peanut butter, and jelly on bread or crackers; cheese-spread on celery or crackers; and icing on cupcakes, graham crackers, or cookies. These opportunities to help prepare snacks should occur often. Let the children cut up the celery or carrots for lunch or a snack. Let them use an egg beater, make the pudding, help mix the corn bread, or stir the Jell–O. Many of the activities from your own kitchen can be brought into the classroom for use in developing the fine motor skills in the children.

You will want to provide a wide variety of puzzles and form boards. These pieces of equipment should range from very easy puzzles, consisting of three or four pieces, to more difficult puzzles, consisting of twenty to twenty-five pieces. At times, you will want to sit down with the children and help them discover how to manipulate the pieces into place. Guide them to select puzzles and form boards which are not too difficult for them and which will allow them to be successful. Encourage the children to try more difficult puzzles as you think they are ready for them, but do not push them beyond their frustration level. Some children will need help with the simplest puzzles.

Choose form boards that include geometric shapes as well as objects such as fruits, vegetables, and animals. The best simple puzzles have individual pieces which are easily identified such as a wing if the puzzle is a bird or a tire if the puzzle is a car.

There are many construction and manipulative toys which you can provide. The size of your budget as well as the range of abilities of the children in your classroom will help determine what you use. Simple nesting and stacking toys will provide the children with the opportunity to take apart and put together at the lowest levels. Toys such as nuts and bolts and simple peg sets are also good for the early levels. As with the puzzles, you will want to sit down with the children and demonstrate to them what can be done with the toy. Stack the blocks together or take the nuts and bolts apart. Children will many times work with a toy longer if someone sits with them. This is an important aspect of the child's experience.

As the children progress through the levels of development, their fine motor skills will enable them to work with construction toys such as Lego, Lincoln Logs, Rings 'N Things, Tinker Toys, and Plexiglass. You can provide many variations of these kinds of equipment. Again, they may need guidance in using the toys, and you may wish to aid in the building. This type of play also lends itself to manipulating small stand-up plastic or wooden toys, such as animals and people, in a type of dramatic play.

The workbench is a valuable piece of equipment which you will want to provide for the development of fine motor skills. Nothing helps the development of eye-hand coordination more than trying to hammer a nail. You will need to show the children how to use the equipment. You may even need to help hold the wood that they are using, but do not hold the nail! As with the art area, let the children use their own ideas and be willing to accept boards nailed together as representing whatever the child says it is.

Providing many shapes and sizes of softwood as well as wooden dowels, wheels, handles, etc., will add to the interest in the woodworking area. This is particularly needed for the higher levels of development where the child is better able to produce his ideas and build what he is thinking about.

Water play and sand play are other activities which foster fine motor skills. You will want to provide utensils for measuring and pouring in both activities. You will want to encourage the children to build in the sand and to make "pies" and "cakes" with the utensils. It does not matter if they spill or drop, and this will allow them to develop the coordination which they will need for handling real food and drinks. The same idea is useful with water play. Provide containers of many different sizes for the children to use. Encourage them to pour from one container to another. This activity builds skill in an atmosphere that is free from concerns about spills and messing up floors. If they need help, show the children how to pour, and talk about what you are doing as you work with the children.

There are some activities with which the children will need help such as hand washing and drying, shoe lacing and tying, buttoning, and zippering. These are individual activities to which you should give attention as the child needs help. Lacing and tying, buttoning, and zippering frames, dolls, or other such apparatus should be a part of your equipment and available for the children to practice on in the room. Since there is no magical age at which children learn to button or tie, provide support until they can do these tasks by themselves. There is often an overlap in time between a child's physical readiness for these tasks and his need for emotional support from a teacher.

Provide many opportunities for the child at the higher levels to copy shapes, numbers, or letters. You can write his ideas down on his art papers, or let him dictate stories to you which he can try to copy *if he is ready and wants to do so.* You will want to provide the child with a model of his name printed in your best manuscript writing so that he can copy from it. (Most handwriting companies provide examples for teachers to use if you do not have any.) At this level, your purpose is to provide good models for the child to copy as he is ready rather than to focus on teaching him to write letters and numbers.

The art activities that you provide can foster the development of cutting with scissors and paper folding. You will want to help the children to learn how to hold the scissors for the best coordination. Working with clay helps to develop muscles in the hands. As you sit with the children, encourage and show them how to roll, squeeze, and manipulate clay. At this stage of development, the manipulation process is as important as the finished product. Encourage the children to use the clay over and over again by giving them rolling pins and cookie cutters. Even those children who can already model objects will enjoy this repeated action in working with clay.

Speech—Sequence of Developmental Behavior

The social or economic levels of families relate directly to a number of speech aspects. These differences appear to be independent of race. Children from higher income levels have better speech sound production, are better able to repeat sentences imitatively, and are better able to understand the sounds of the spoken language than children from lower income levels. Higher ability on these aspects of speech are also positively related to general intelligence. It is not fully known what is the cause and effect in these observations. However, it is known that children of low income backgrounds learn speech from language users who often use nonstandard English and who may use a somewhat different set of speech sounds; yet, their speech is judged by standard English usage. Also, the measurement of intelligence is partly dependent upon these same social class differences.

After infancy, the child eventually produces the sounds which he hears. For this reason, auditory discrimination of speech sounds always precedes their production in the course of normal development. Difficulties of hearing will affect both sound discrimination and speech production. If a child has difficulty in these areas, it is wise to have his hearing checked. We need to be careful not to confuse speech differences which result from social class or general intelligence with differences which are specific to the hearing and sound production process. A speech and hearing specialist can be helpful with such matters, or a psychological consultation may be needed.

In general, speech levels have not been as extensively established as they have been for the gross and fine motor areas. Only that information on which you can rely is included here. Children with specific motor development difficulties and those who have some defect in the formation or operation of their speech mechanisms (i.e., lips, tongue, hard and soft palate, teeth, voice box, nasal passageway or breath control) will show speech patterns which differ from the normal development sequences.

For your convenience, if something is known about each of these areas within the various levels, it is presented in this order: efficiency of speech sound reception (auditory discrimination or auditory reception), ability to imitate sentences, and speech sounds which the child produces (articulation). The way in which these areas are measured influences the extent to which children of a given developmental level will be successful. For this reason, you will be told the conditions under which a certain observation is obtained.

Level I.   At this level, auditory reception is poor. Exact percentages have not been determined, but it is clear that a child of normal hearing and development may understand at any moment only one-half or less of the speech sounds which he hears. This means that he is quite dependent upon the context in which things are said and upon the repetition of things until he understands them.

No direct evidence is available regarding the child's ability to imitate the language of an adult or child. From the evidence available at level III, it is safe to assume that the level I child's ability is far lower. He can perhaps imitate a three to four word simple sentence such as "The doggie is there" or "This is candy," although as at all developmental levels, his spontaneous speech may sometimes exceed the level which he will imitate.

In his spontaneous speech or during his repetition of single words, the child will probably produce most of the vowel sounds. It is not fully predictable which consonant sounds will be used, since this depends very much on what sounds his parents have tried to have him produce. When they have placed an emphasis on *B, P, M, W,* or *H,* the child may be able to produce them. They may also have encouraged *T, D,* or *N* to the extent that the child will also produce them. However, the absence of any of these consonant sounds is not yet a cause for concern. The child of this level will rely on pointing, tugging, and pulling the adult or fussing to make his point.

Level II. Auditory reception is still much like that described for level I, with slight improvement. One might expect a single word comprehension level to approach 50 percent. Again, no direct evidence is available regarding sentence repetition, although this can be expected to have improved quite a bit over level I.

The consonants which the child uses still heavily reflect family speech patterns toward the child. The probability of hearing all of the consonants listed under level I has increased.

Level III. It is estimated that the child discriminates between 55 and 65 percent of the English speech sounds which he hears, with reference to their appearance in single words. That is, if a word is spoken to him out of a sentence context (provided that the words are words with which he is familiar), he will be able to indicate an understanding of the word by pointing to a picture or by deciding whether similar sounding words that are presented together in pairs are the same or not.

His ability to repeat simple sentences with no more than one word substituted or missing (not counting articulation difficulties) is with 30 to 75 percent accuracy, averaging about 50 percent. Sentence forms which he is most likely to repeat correctly are illustrated by the following examples: Fish swim. (subject-verb); Tommy drinks water. (subject-verb-object); He bumped the bed very hard. (subject-verb-object-adverbial modifier of verb); The child is running to Mama. (subject-verb-prepositional phrase modifier of verb); Bobby was driven to the lake. (subject-passive verb-prepositional phrase modifier of verb); Teacher told me to go home. (subject-verb-indirect object-infinitive-adverbial modifier of infinitive).

At this level, we expect particular consonant sounds will be present, although not necessarily perfectly formed. We expect *M, N,*

H, W, P, J (as in junior), *CH* (as in chip), *S* (possibly lisped), and we may hear *Z, TR* (as in train), *BL* (as in black). In these last two, we commonly hear the *W* substituted (as in t*w*ain and b*w*ack). Those who know the child well will sometimes have difficulty understanding him and will need to ask questions to clarify what he has said.

Level IV.   Auditory discrimination has improved to 65 to 75 percent accuracy, so the child is more likely to understand what is said than he was at level III.

The child now repeats in imitation 50 to 85 percent correctly, with an average rate of perhaps 65 percent, for sentences like those listed in level III and for sentences like: All of those branches touched him. (subject-prepositional phrase-verb-object). Such a tiny car is coming; (subject modifier-subject-verb). Remember that the child does this well and shows auditory discrimination accuracy when you have his undivided attention; however, he probably misses a lot more of what people say when he is busy playing or otherwise distracted.

We now expect the child to be able to say *B, F, G, K,* and probably *T* and *D.* The diphthongs *OU* (as in ouch) and *OI* (as in oil) will probably appear in the child's speech, although approximately correct forms are considered quite developmentally normal.

Level V.   Auditory discrimination may now be 70 to 80 percent correct. The child's ability to imitate easy sentences has risen to perhaps 65 to 90 percent accuracy. This applies to sentence types listed for levels III and IV and for sentences such as: He thought you wanted the toy. (subject-verb-subject of dependent clause-verb-object); Her horse started before she could catch it. (subject modifier-subject-verb-conjunction-subject-verb-object); If she's there, he wants to hurry. (conjunction-subject-contracted verb-adverb-subject-verb-infinitive).

The sounds *F* and *V* are probably articulated. From level IV, *K* and *G* are firmly established but give the child trouble when they appear in blends (e.g., *G* sound in *g*rouch or *K* sound in *c*risp). *TH, NG,* and *Y* (as in un*i*on) may be present. This is the first level at which we expect the child to be reasonably understandable to a stranger. By the end of this level, some children will be using *L, CH, SH, ZH, R,* and other difficult blends. Many children will be omitting these sounds, but they will nevertheless be entirely understandable.

SPEECH OBJECTIVES FOR PRESCHOOL-AGED CHILDREN

1. To produce speech which is understood by a stranger.
2. To correctly reproduce consonant sounds and blends (i.e., *M, N, H, W, P, J* as in junior, *CH, S, B, Z, TR, BL, F, G K, T,* and dipthongs *OU, OI*). The child may have trouble with *K* and *G* when they appear in blends. *TH, NG,* and *Y* as in un*io*n may be present.

WHAT THE TEACHER DOES

The most important thing you can do as a teacher is to model the correct speech sounds in your own speech. Most children will learn to make the speech sounds as they hear them. A few children need help in shaping speech by many repetitions and confirmations. Talk to children not only so they will hear speech sounds but also in such a way that they will want to respond. Talk about whatever is of special interest to the child (e.g., what happened on the way to school, a baby brother, a pet, his birthday, any special event). The practice that the teacher provides should be talking in general as a model rather than specific practice with specific sounds, particularly with children who are at the lower developmental levels. The purpose is imitation, not drill. As children approach levels IV and V, they enjoy poems and stories with nonsense sounds; and they may enjoy stories built around a special letter or sound, especially if humor is built into the story and if there is an opportunity for the children to participate by repeating certain words or sounds along with you as the story is read. If you have children with articulation problems, simple activities such as beating a drum while pronouncing the child's name will help him to hear syllables and distinguish sounds. Saying a child's name as a ball is thrown to him or an object is passed to him in a small group will also help him to be aware of speech sounds.

You can be particularly helpful to the child by providing many listening experiences, especially after he has reached level III. There are excellent records that deal with noises and where they happen which encourage the child to listen for the noise and guess what it is. Opportunities to listen to stories and records should be provided daily; a "listening post" with stories recorded by the teacher encourages children to listen. A tape recorder can be used to encourage both listening and talking. Your awareness of sound and your ability to make the children aware of sounds around them will help to give them auditory practice and an interest in sound.

As a general rule, do not call attention to the sounds which the child does not pronounce correctly. You may find it necessary to have a child repeat what he has said in order to understand it, but try to do this as inconspicuously as possible.

Growth and Maturation

In this section, instead of referring to levels, we state the exact ages at which certain growth signs are expected. This is done because deviations from expected growth patterns, unlike grouped behavior patterns, are useful only in this way. It is important to keep records of each child's height, weight, and head circumference throughout the preschool period. If major changes appear which possibly reflect upon his health and well-being, they can be interpreted. For example, your impression that a child is overly short, tall, thin, or heavy is best understood by comparing his current height and weight to what they were at an earlier age. Ideally, each child's height and weight will both be high or both be medium or both be low for his chronological age. Taller children should be heavier, and shorter children lighter.

Through the years of early childhood, the child's body gradually changes in proportion. His head grows most slowly, his legs grow most rapidly, and his body grows at an intermediate rate. His face grows more rapidly than the rest of his head. The result is that the child's legs become larger in proportion to the rest of his body; he changes from a stubby appearing toddler into a more slender appearing child. His abdominal muscles are weak until the beginning of early childhood so his tummy hangs out. As his strength and balance increase, you will notice that his abdominal muscles begin to pull this bulge in.

Adequate nutrition and rest are essential to normal growth and maturation. The body chemicals which stimulate growth and tissue rebuilding are released during certain stages of sleep. The child who always misses sleep will be affected in his growth. Children from low income families often receive too little protein, B complex, vitamin C, and iron, and some receive too few calories, although some children will be overweight from receiving too many calories while still lacking the essential ingredients for healthy, balanced growth. Frequently, children from low income families will be deficient in calcium and vitamin A. Family and subcultural food preferences strongly affect dietary balance, sometimes as much as does income level. Food preferences of children closely resemble those of their families. Any marked deficiency in total caloric intake is potentially damaging to the child's health, even more so than a shortage of vitamins, and may lead to growth retardation and mental retardation. It does not follow from this that excess calories are beneficial—they are not. Excesses of vitamins A and D may, in fact, be harmful.

As a general principle, the child's length at birth is positively related to his height at six years of age. Height is affected by the child's heredity more than weight is. Environmental factors do influence height somewhat; however, they have a greater influence on weight. Environment can only prevent the child from attaining his full potential in height, but it cannot increase this potential. Excess calories, on the other hand, will increase the child's potential lifelong weight just as surely as too few calories will have the undesirable effects which were already mentioned. The potential for being of low, medium, or average weight is almost irreversibly established in infancy and early childhood by total caloric intake. An average early childhood weight is later associated with the ability to lose excess weight easily, but a heavy early childhood weight is later associated with extreme difficulty in losing weight. The child who has a shortage of protein, calcium, and vitamin D will grow up to be shorter than he would have been under normal circumstances. From these facts, it is easy to understand why low income children tend on the average to be shorter, lighter, and to have smaller head circumferences than children from more affluent homes. These latter children may suffer from overnutrition. What is desirable is adequate, balanced nutrition for every child. Early childhood programs bear an important responsibility in this area. The following norms will help you in your efforts to carry out this responsibility.

Any time that you find a child has changed a large amount in his relative standing on any of these measures, you should find some satisfactory explanation for the change. You may wish to refer the parents to a physician. Any child who is excessively light or heavy for his height should be checked by a physician. Furthermore, any child whose height or weight falls outside the limits which include 94 percent of all children or whose head circumference falls outside the limits which include 96 percent of all children should be examined, unless a diagnosis has already been established. Children

	*	HEIGHT (inches)		WEIGHT (pounds)	
		Girls	Boys	Girls	Boys
36 Months	94%	34½–40½	35½–40½	25½–42	27–39
	80%	35½–39½	36–39½	27½–37½	28½–37·
	Average	37½	37½	32	32½
48 Months	94%	37½–44½	38½–43½	29–48	30–44½
	80%	38½–43	39–42½	31–43	32–42
	Average	40½	40½	36	36½
60 Months	94%	40–47	40½–46½	32–52	34–52
	80%	41–45½	41½–46	35–49	36½–48½
	Average	43	43½	41	42
72 Months	94%	42½–49½	43–50	37–59	38½–61
	80%	43½–48	44–48½	40–54	41–56½
	Average	45½	46½	47	48

		HEAD CIRCUMFERENCE (inches)	
		Girls	Boys
36 Months	96%	18¼–20¼	18¾–20¾
	Average	19½	19¾
48 Months	96%	18½–20¾	19–21
	Average	19¾	20
60 Months	96%	18¾–20¾	19–21¼
	Average	19¾	20
72 Months	96%	19–20¾	19–21¼
	Average	20	20¼

*These are the limits within which 94%, 80%, and 96% of all children fall. Average means the 50th percentile.

whose height or weight differs from 80 percent of the population but does not exceed the 94 percent limits should be watched. If it cannot be explained by family size, other checks should be made. Finally, any child who is exceedingly small may be having growth problems. It will be helpful for you to have the advice of a qualified nutritionist in these matters.

GROWTH AND MATURATION GUIDES FOR PRESCHOOL-AGED CHILDREN

These guides provide information for teachers rather than state the specific behavior on the part of the child. The major responsibility for providing the conditions which are necessary to physical growth is usually considered primarily within the realm of family responsibilities. However, school responsibility may differ considerably from one program to another; for example, full day programs and programs for children from low income families may take more responsibility for the growth needs of the children than do half-day programs.

1. To keep accurate information regarding the child's height, weight, and head circumference in order to show the pattern of growth.
2. To provide proper conditions for rest and activity.
3. To provide for good nutrition and eating habits.
4. To help parents understand the importance of proper maturation and growth.

WHAT THE TEACHER DOES

Someone in the school should make accurate physical measures of the children at regular intervals. A nurse or physician can show you how to take these measures properly. These records should be studied by the person who is responsible for the medical aspects of the program to reveal any deviations from the normal growth pattern. Arrangements should be made with the family to consult their family doctor or the school physician for the needed examinations and treatment.

The school personnel should be alert to the effect of the school environment on the health needs of the children. Policies should be developed and maintained which will assure a healthful and safe environment for the children. This includes the provision that all adults who are in direct contact with the children will also be in good physical and mental health.

As the classroom teacher, you should maintain a balance between activity and rest in the program. Sometimes this requires a consciousness of the needs of individual children. The total schedule should provide times when the children are encouraged to vary their activity; keep in mind that young children are seldom quiet and still for more than a few minutes at a time and that some children are very easily overstimulated in a group situation and may need encouragement to find something quiet to do. If you are aware of the needs of the individual children in the class, you can often create a change in the balance of activity by the materials that you put out or put away at a particular time. If you think that the children are tired of being active, sometimes just sitting down with a book will attract the children to listen quietly to a story. If the children seem to be tired of building with blocks, a quiet game may provide the needed change. If the children are tired of listening to a story, some rhythms or mimicry may provide the chance to move around and be actively involved.

If the school does serve food, the main meal should be served in the middle of the day; snacks should be provided in midmorning and midafternoon. If the food is well prepared and attractively served, how well the children eat and how they feel about mealtime at school will be largely dependent on how well the mealtime is guided by the teachers. If you want the children to eat the food, you must eat it yourself and you must make mealtime a pleasant experience. Children respond well to such techniques as helping themselves to new foods, helping themselves to seconds, and taking empty plates to a table to get dessert. They do not respond well to coaxing or to being hurried. Mealtime should be a pleasant social situation; however, remember that younger children have more difficulty when attempting to eat and talk at the same time. While you should not stop the talking, you may need to keep it from taking too much attention from the eating.

Schools that do not serve meals can help children understand more about foods and nutrition by providing them with the opportunity to prepare various fruits and vegetables which can be eaten by the children at snack time. You can plan cooking experiences which enable them to participate in the preparation of nutritious puddings, fruit dishes, and simple sandwiches. Despite the fact that sweets will usually be well received by the children, they should not always prepare cake and candy.

As you work with parents, remember to include those topics which will help them understand what they can do to contribute to the best growth of their children. Often there are concerns among the staff or the parents that provide the beginning place. Sometimes there are children in the group who have eating problems. Parents are often concerned about nose and throat disorders that are so common among young children, or they wonder whether they should have their children's eyes tested. Do not be surprised if parents are concerned about some things which take place at school; for example, the parents might be concerned about what is served at the snack time or the safety of the children. Be prepared to study these aspects of the program. Learning other people's conception of the situation may give you some new insights.

chapter 5

Helping Children to Develop Cognitive Skills

Cognitive skills relate to those behaviors which reveal what the child knows; that is, how the child processes, stores, and comprehends information about the environment, and how he responds to and uses such information to interact with the environment. For this age range, there are seven general aspects of cognitive behavior which have been studied extensively and may be helpful to consider when planning for the child. They are attention, perception, memory, concepts, language and gestures, mediation, and problem solving and logical thought.

Attention refers to the child's tendency to direct his regard toward something. The child's distribution of attention is related to the novelty and familiarity of particular features, events, or meanings in the environment. Attention is sometimes an involuntary or automatic process; for example, the child's attention is attracted by a sudden movement or a loud noise, or the child no longer attends to a repetitious, monotonous happening. Attention is sometimes voluntary or directed; for example, the child looks at something after being requested to do so, or he continues to do some task which may or may not be interesting. The child's ability to maintain attention is often referred to as his *attention span,* implying that this is a voluntary process only. No absolute statements can be made about the attention span for tasks in general because its duration depends on whether the child's attention is voluntary or involuntary and on his motivation to interact with the task. When motivation is positive for a task, the child will appear to have a long attention span; this action reveals little information about his capacity for voluntary attention. The reverse is true as well. For this reason, we can determine a child's best attention span when he is performing a task which is motivating for him.

Perception refers to the child's experience of recognizing or knowing what reaches him through his senses. For instance, when a child sees an airplane and recognizes it as an airplane, we say he perceives it. If he sees an airplane for the first time or fails to recognize what it is, he may point to it in excitement and jabber about the "thing" which is creating sensory impressions on him; in this case, he does not perceive. For convenience perceptual behavior is divided into groups that are associated with vision, hearing, and other senses; the emphasis is placed upon recognition as the evidence that perception has occurred.

Memory refers to the child's storage capacity or his ability to retain information. Although behaviors which relate to memory are discussed separately from those which relate to attention and perception, you will want to maintain the perspective that these three groups of behavior are not independent of each other. On the contrary, they are closely interrelated. That is, things which interfere with a child's attention will often make his memory appear dull, or a disturbance of perception can interfere with memory or attention.

Concepts are ideas about groupings or classes of things or events. For example, if we talk about *past events,* that is a concept or an idea which groups together all of those events which happened before the present. *All of the red things* is another concept. Concepts may be made more complicated or difficult than this by placing further limits on the things or events to be included in the grouping. The last example would become more complicated if we grouped together all of the *round,* red things. Now the group includes only those things which are both *red* and *round.* Children find these doubly limited concepts to be more complicated and difficult. The concept would be even more difficult if the group consisted of small, round, red things.

Technically, children at levels I through III do not experience true concepts; instead they have what the Swiss psychologist, Jean Piaget, has called *preconcepts*. The child forms true concepts at levels IV and V. You will understand more fully from the descriptions in the final section of this chapter how preconcepts are less mature ideas than concepts.

Language and gestures are those communicative behaviors which would normally belong in this section. We have, however, placed the motor aspects of language, that is speech, in the preceding chapter. In the case of language, the teacher is concerned with what the child understands and how he expresses himself. Both of these aspects are examined in this section of the present chapter.

The two remaining areas of behavior are more difficult to understand. This may be because they refer to the operations which occur within the child's thinking processes. Therefore, they are more difficult to observe and, likewise, more difficult to understand. Nevertheless, mediation and problem solving and logical thought are important aspects of the child's development. We will try to look at these aspects of the child's behavior in the hope that doing so will bring us closer to our central task of understanding the individual child as he is experiencing things. By understanding what and how he is experiencing, we will be better equipped to communicate, relate, and provide developmentally useful experiences.

Mediation is something in thought which happens between events. Something often does happen in the child's thinking between the time he perceives an event and the time that he reacts to it with some observable response. If these mediational events could be seen directly by us, we would often understand why the child reacts as he does. Specifically, we will refer to the in-between events as mediations whenever they show that an association exists for the child between an original observable event plus its meaning and an internal response to it which affects how the child responds. The observable event plus its meaning leads to an association or mediation which in turn leads to the observable behavior which we see.

The mediational association may be an understandable one; for example, a child becomes angry in response to someone calling him a name. This angry response results from some mediation. Because children have different mediations, we cannot predict how a child, who is unknown to us, might mediate and hence react to name calling. How he would react would depend upon his mediation. Another child might show fear and withdrawal after being called a name while another might respond saying, "Sticks and stones may hurt . . ." and so forth. Mediation is not the same thing as comprehension of the act of name calling. In all three of our examples,

comprehension appears to be present. Something more than comprehension has taken place between the name calling and the child's
response to it and that something is mediation.

When we believe that we understand a child's mediations, we say
that we understand his behavior; yet many times we cannot imagine
what a child is thinking so we cannot understand his reactions to the
stimulus events which he experiences. In the latter circumstance,
we often search for an explanation of why a child behaves as he does.
This clearly seems to be a search for the child's mediations. Young
children's mediations are difficult for us to understand because (1)
they are private in the sense that the child has not acquired a fully
socialized ability to express his associations through language, (2)
they result from the child's personal history (i.e., they are not immediately apparent unless we are fully familiar with that history as it
pertains to present circumstances), and (3) adults have forgotten
how they might have mediated when they were of a similar age.

Problem solving and logical thought are types of mediative behaviors. These include the strategies that the child may use to solve
problems; the child's overall understanding of reality, which may be
characteristic of his developmental level rather than peculiar to his
·personal associations; and other higher mental processes which are
typical of his age. Strictly speaking, all behavior in this age range
is prelogical thought so the use of the term *logical thought* draws
attention to the designated behaviors which are the forerunners of
logic.

Problem solving sometimes requires the use of concepts on which
the child operates in some purposeful way. Language may be used
by the child in his problem-solving operations, although imitation
and other actions including some internal actions of imagination
may also be used. Unlike mediations, which seem to result from the
child's unique history of life experiences, problem-solving behaviors
and logical thought tend to be common to many of the children who
are of the same developmental level.

Attention—Sequence of Developmental Behavior

Level I.   At this level, attention is less a voluntary than an involuntary act. To maintain a child's attention, you must find the combination of stimulus conditions which will most effectively hold his
interest. The child shows attention to exploring his immediate environment (e.g., opening cupboard doors and taking things out). Touch

is an important channel of attention regulation. Visually, the child will attend to pictures, colored blocks, and the actions of others. This last fact is one secret of getting the child to try new things because what can be observed may be imitated (e.g., a crayon stroke or a form board placement demonstration). Brief, simple stories about familiar things, repetitious sounds from books or in rhymes, and the child's own sound productions and repetitions of them regulate his attention. In general, these experiences are all relatively less novel than those which will later hold the child's attention.

Level II.   The child's environmental exploration continues and widens in scope. Repetition and familiarity are, however, still hallmarks of his attention. He turns through the pages of a book of picture stories, attends briefly to his immediate memory of something from which he has been distracted by an external event, and may tear things apart in the process of examining them. Behavior is easily encouraged by demonstration. For example, he completes simple block constructions in imitation, and he adapts his orientation to a form board which he has been working after one or two trials when an adult demonstrates the new format. Not only can he benefit from an example but he also more clearly behaves on instruction than formerly. He attends to forms and form boards on request, and he continues until ten forms have been placed in a form board as long as the adult continues to watch him. It is as if the child learns to pay attention from the adult's example of paying attention to him. The imitative theme plays a part in his initial participation at this level in group activities such as ring-around-the-rosy. The child's attention span is longer than before; he now concentrates on placing many small pellets into a narrow-mouthed bottle. The continuing role of touch and action perhaps explains in part why the pellet-bottle and form board tasks produce long attentional performances.

The familiar is comfortable, and the child is wary of dark places and unfamiliar things. The child's attention will be vigilant in the face of such threatening experiences. Positive attention is maintained by the following activities: repetition of rhymes, a familiar story told over and over, talking about himself, hearing a song again and again, and hearing musical instruments or records repeatedly. A new story is decidedly less appealing to the child.

Level III.   The child's visual attention remains impulsive in that distractors effectively capture it. The child explores a wider and wider environment. Even though he shows more exploratory eye movements than before, they are poorly coordinated. He does better at maintaining attention when both touch and action are involved. He will, for example, attend for an interval to sorting black and white buttons, assembling things, and drawing or painting. He performs simple block constructions from a model which he has not seen constructed, so he is less dependent upon viewing the actions of an adult. On request, he shows a sufficient amount of attention to describe a picture as long as someone is listening. He adapts more quickly than before to a reversal of a form board. It appears that a curiosity to understand things is beginning to guide his attention. Familiar stories continue to be favored; however, new stories now appeal to him. He attends to the physical qualities of his own voice (i.e., rate and loudness) while he is speaking. His greater ability to attend to his own behavior is reflected by his attention to his memory of events when he is telling an experience. He also begins to describe his own actions while in the process of performing them which contributes to the growth of imaginative play.

Level IV. The child continues to have impulsive, distractible visual attention. His exploratory eye movements increase and become slightly more organized. The child pays better attention to details of the human body; his drawings of human figures are more detailed. (Attention should be distinguished from perception in this case because perception has reached this level of attainment before this time.) He watches an adult folding a paper and imitates the operation on request.

His voluntary aspects of attention are increasing; he gives the impression that his span of attention has appreciably improved. He obeys directions which require him to attend to something, and he acts upon commands containing simple prepositions (e.g., in, on, under, beside). When relating events to others, he is less likely than before to be distracted. Attention to experiential elements within his memory allow him to tell a coherent story which places events in a correct order.

Level V. The child's visual attention is better organized and less impulsive than before. Touch is declining in importance for maintaining attention. He moves freely about the house, yard, and immediate neighborhood outside his mother's immediate observation. His drawings of human figures show a clear differentiation of head and body, and he completes an incomplete man in essential respects. When asked to tell everything about a picture, his attention directs him to mention several of the things in the picture (i.e., he enumerates them). Despite this progress, he is still subject to overly concentrating on some limited aspect of what he experiences to the exclusion of other aspects; or if he shifts his attention to another aspect, he is inclined to lose track of that to which he previously attended. However, when two aspects can be handled in sequence, he can attend first to one and then the other. Thus, when he is given a complex question which requires two different answers, he will give attention to one and then to the other. His auditory attention is sufficient to permit him to tap simple rhythms after hearing them; he is showing auditory-motor coordination.

ATTENTION OBJECTIVES FOR
PRESCHOOL-AGED CHILDREN

1. To direct attention to one activity of interest even though other activities are possible.
2. To redirect attention from one object to another.
3. To voluntarily focus on an appropriate activity or piece of equipment when requested to do so by the teacher (not before level IV).

WHAT THE TEACHER DOES

Our concern is with the involuntary and voluntary aspects of attention in relation to two kinds of situations; namely, those in which the child chooses his own activities and those in which the child attends to activities which are planned by the teacher. You cannot teach attention, but you can teach in such a way that the development of attention is facilitated. A child's attention span increases when he has something to do that is interesting.

You focus upon involuntary aspects of attention when you place an interesting object or toy where a child will see it, imitate the sound of a train when reading a story, or insert the child's name in a question or use it in a song. These techniques are effective with the youngest children. Sometimes you sit on the floor by the blocks and start to stack them or line them up, and a child joins you in the activity. As several children join you and seem to be capable of building independently, you may stay near and give only the help which is needed to keep the activity going. Some children who are overstimulated in a group need a quiet corner in which to play—

maybe with only one quiet, cooperative child. You require the child's voluntary attention when you expect him to sit with a group and listen to a story, to participate in routines, to put on his coat and boots, or to put away toys.

The distinction between the child's attention to self-chosen activities and teacher-chosen activities is an important one. With three- and four-year-old children, the emphasis is on increasing the time that they will attend to activities which are self-chosen. The program must be organized so opportunities are available to make choices for a major portion of the child's time. Ordinarily, the work period, free play time, and the outdoor time provide time for this activity. To be successful, you must plan new and interesting activities. Materials which have lost their appeal should be removed from the room. Teachers should encourage the children to continue activities which they have begun. For example, if a table has been prepared for the use of pottery clay, it is helpful if you sit at the table, pat and roll a piece of clay, and talk with the children about what they are doing. (Avoid making specific animals, etc. If you do things that are beyond the abilities of the children, their immediate response will be, "Make me one." You only want to show the children what they could do.) Allow the children to move freely from one activity to another, but give special attention to children who flit from one activity to another without settling down to anything.

Some teacher-directed activities are necessary to maintain routines, but the teacher's expectations should be within the range of the child's ability. For example, toys have to be put away, but the children grow from helping a little to taking a major responsibility. Younger children cannot concentrate on putting away blocks for a long period; a few blocks are put away, and they start playing again unless their attention is redirected and help is given. Older preschoolers can cooperatively do the job with little help and direction.

When listening to a story in a group, the child is required to integrate the visual and auditory aspects of attention; he also needs to resist the distraction of other children. You can gather four or five children together and read to them; at first, it is wise to postpone a story group for all of the children until they can listen without constant appeals for order. At first, stories must be short and appealing to the children. Continue to read only as long as the children are willing to listen. Little or nothing is gained by forcing children in a group activity before they have learned to enjoy the activity.

Some general teaching techniques are helpful in developing the children's attention spans. When you speak to a child, be sure you have his attention. Some children, even by the age of three, have learned to tune out what adults say to them. Try to get eye-to-eye contact with the children, and do not talk to them as long as they are talking to each other or obviously playing with each other. To gain his attention, gently touch the child on the hand, face, or head. Sometimes a pause or a reminder that you are waiting for their attention will help. Establish a visual signal such as raising your hand. If you make a practice of expecting attention, children will respond.

Avoid repeating what you have told children. Children can learn not to listen the first time because they know you will repeat it several times. Repeat if the children do not understand, but keep directions simple. Avoid a lot of needless talk so that directions do not have to be separated from chatter.

Success is essential to the development of attention. A young child's persistence at an activity which he cannot do is very short. If you see that a child is having difficulty, offer enough assistance so that he will be successful before he becomes discouraged and stops or angry enough to destroy his work. Activities should be challenging but not frustrating. Help the child to enjoy his successes. Let him know how you feel by a word of praise, a smile, or a word of encouragement. Giving the child recognition or praise causes him to continue what he is doing.

The child's motivation cannot be overlooked since it has an effect upon his attention span. This subject is discussed at length in Chapter Six.

Perception—Sequence of Developmental Behavior

Level I.   The child recognizes familiar adults from photographs and his own image in the mirror. He is beginning to overcome the impression of things as wholes; he recognizes many simple line drawings of objects when the ones to be identified are placed among sets of quite different (and thus nonconfusing) objects; he recognizes fine details in favorite pictures in a storybook; he perceives familiar objects after seeing only parts of them (throughout this age range, his development of recognition for out-of-focus pictures is quite similar to that for recognition of objects from parts); and he is barely able to locate an object which has been concealed against an unfamiliar background (e.g., the picture of a dog concealed in the leaves of a tree).

A similar trend is developing in the child's hearing. He is beginning to recognize the sounds which go together to make words. He should be able, for example, to recognize the word *milk* when it is pronounced as several separate sounds (i.e., *m..il..k*) if a picture is available to provide supporting cues or associations for this perception. Likewise, he can perceive separately and repeat a word when requested to do so. For example, when he is asked, "Now listen. Say *dog,*" he will sort out the word *dog,* perceiving it separately as the word to be repeated and say, *"Dog."* He repeats word sequences (e.g., "He is running" or "On the chair") when requested to do so. He perceives larger language units, such as a question, well enough to attempt an answer. The child's ability to perceive the inflection of the questioner raising his or her voice to indicate the question mark at the end of the sentence is essential to his perception of the common form of the English question. The first direct evidence of the child's perception of rhythm in music often appears at this level in his swaying motions. He depends upon hearing all of the sounds of a word before he recognizes it; this suggests that the perceptual skill of recognizing wholes from parts may appear later in hearing than in vision. The child thus depends upon careful articulation of words by others.

Level II. The child recognizes a photograph of himself (assuming that he has had prior experience with mirrors), miniature objects as being equivalent perceptually to their real counterparts, colors, and tiny details of drawings. His drawing discrimination is better; he will select an object from among other drawings which are closer competitors than at level I. His perception of form is sufficient for the correct placement of most simple geometric forms in a form board in a brief period of time (it is no longer a matter of slow trial-and-error placement). The child's ability to find concealed objects in pictures is only slightly improved. The child possesses little perceptual skill in hearing. His perception of single words which are spoken out of context is quite immature, but he recognizes more words in a speech context or when visual cues are present. He can perceive a compound sentence of familiar words, and he can demonstrate his comprehension of the sentence. Recognizing words with missing sounds is still very difficult.

Level III. The child recognizes more colors although he may confuse blue and green. He can place objects in a form board much more rapidly. He assembles simple puzzles, recognizes animals which look alike and matches them, points out a particular animal's picture from among a set of different animals, sorts black and white objects, and recognizes a substantial number of pictures of objects and actions from among some close competitors or among relatively unfamiliar objects for which he probably does not know the names. His vision and hearing are more coordinated, as demonstrated by his ability to supply names for many pictured objects. His ability to find concealed objects against unfamiliar backgrounds is increasing. He begins to select the heavier of two objects, showing another discrimination ability. His recognition has not improved for words that are pronounced with each sound emphasized but separated by pauses. In contrast, the child is much better at recognizing words from which a sound has been omitted. The latter involves less sequential perception, which probably accounts for it being less difficult.

Level IV. The child recognizes incomplete forms (e.g., ship, cat, telephone) about two-thirds as well as he will recognize them at the end of the elementary school years. His ability to find concealed objects continues to improve. He can match all of the primary colors correctly. He assembles simple puzzles much faster. The child distinguishes the front from the back of his clothing, stacks graduated blocks (from larger to smaller), demonstrates some silhouette matching skills (these provide less detail than line drawings), and discriminates which person's picture is pretty. He can nearly always correctly select the heavier of two weights. He recognizes more difficult words with missing sounds and begins to perceive, without the supportive picture cues, those words which are pronounced with sounds separated by pauses.

Level V. Going a step beyond the simple puzzle, the child can arrange into a picture parts whose sides are all straight and regular, and thus provide no shape cues for fitting. He can spot and point out major missing details of familiar objects. He can assemble difficult puzzles which have no color or shading cues, and he can copy very simple mosaic tile or block designs or bead designs. He recognizes a penny, nickel, and dime. The child matches as many as ten to twelve colors, ties a single knot around a stick (showing a complicated perception of the relation of the ends of the string), forms a rectangle or a square from two triangular pieces, and has skills in matching silhouettes. Seeing concealed forms is perhaps at over 50 percent of the skill level that the child will have at the end of childhood. The foregoing observations suggest a greater constancy of form and a better perceptual grasp of how parts can make larger wholes without the child requiring the amount of detail which was formerly necessary to permit similar levels of performance. That is, his perception has become more abstract from real objects. However, if a picture is placed in an unusual orientation, such as upside down or in a quite unfamiliar context, it will be difficult for the child to distinguish an object. These difficulties may relate to perceptual habits that are characteristic at this level. It is known, for example, that a visual scanning pattern of top-to-bottom search becomes prominent at this level; perhaps this accounts for the problem of recognizing objects which are turned upside down or rotated. These positional changes force the child to take in information in a sequence that is different from the sequence that he normally uses, thus making it difficult for him to compare the information to the information that he has stored internally.

The child perceives more words whose sounds are separated by pauses and words with missing sounds. These events reveal developments in hearing which parallel those that were discussed for vision. Nevertheless, at this level, the child's visual perception is developmentally ahead of his hearing perception, and the combination of the two is more satisfactory than either alone.

PERCEPTION OBJECTIVES FOR PRESCHOOL-AGED CHILDREN

1. To recognize new objects.
2. To recognize characteristics which distinguish one animate or inanimate object from another.
3. To hear and understand separate sounds and sound combinations (i.e., words, phrases, sentences).
4. To recognize something after seeing only part of it.
5. To recognize familiar objects from pictures.

WHAT THE TEACHER DOES

This section points out the importance of providing experiences through which the child may use his senses to acquire information. Opportunities for many visual, auditory, tactile, and taste experiences are in order. Visual experiences make up an appreciable part of the early childhood program (i.e., experiences with color; shape;

all kinds of inanimate objects such as cars, trains, airplanes, buildings, toys, furnishings, containers, utensils, plants, fruits, vegetables, money; and animate objects such as mammals, birds, insects, fish, and people). You can ask what is new in our room today. You can provide the opportunity for the child to view objects, to comment on his observations, and to ask questions about what he observed. In relation to visual perception, it is appropriate for you to ask questions such as: What color is it? How does it move? What is it called? What can it do? What does it eat? In relation to auditory perception, it is appropriate for you to ask questions such as: What noise does it make? What does it sound like? In relation to tactile perception, it is appropriate for you to ask: How does it feel? Is it hard (soft)? Is it rough (smooth)? In relation to taste, you might ask: How does it taste? Can you eat it? Whatever the child does not know, you can help him to understand. Sometimes you will need to answer your own question, but frequently what one child perceives can be used to help another child learn.

Emphasis should be placed on providing experiences with real objects, yet children's experiences need not all be with real objects. They enjoy pictures, especially large, colorful pictures of things with which they are familiar. A small collection of pictures mounted in scrapbook form can provide an opportunity for one or two children and an adult to look at it and talk about what is there. A larger picture that is mounted and placed on a wall or bulletin board, low where the children can see it and point to objects while discussing them, is also attractive, especially if the picture is changed fairly often. Gradually, children will be able to recognize familiar things from pictures, but they will not learn to recognize unfamiliar things from seeing a picture.

You can discuss the children's observations of pictures in relation to stories that are real, listen for sounds on records, talk about different sounds that they hear on the way to school, and listen for sounds in the classroom. Playing with sound can be fun. You can shake some beans or rice in a small sealed box to determine the sound that they will make. Older preschool children enjoy playing with sounds that rhyme or words that begin with the same sound as their name. Children can play simple guessing games that you make up that are based on sound, but in the classroom you usually do not use such things as words with missing sounds. Exercises of the latter type are used more for testing situations. In the classroom you usually concentrate on providing an opportunity for children to hear words, phrases, and sentences that are used in a meaningful context.

This is how the children will learn to understand words. You can create games in which only a part of a familiar object is revealed and have the children guess what the object is. These guessing games are more successful with only four or five children because everyone wants an opportunity to guess without having to wait for a turn.

Memory—Sequence of Developmental Behavior

Earlier comments that were made in the perception section regarding the child's ability to perceive words from which sounds have been omitted apply here. That is, the same levels of behavior indicate something about both memory and perception. In regard to memory, these behaviors imply the extent to which the child has a word memory that is sufficient for him to reconstruct the whole word from only some of its parts. This same interpretation also applies to the memory and perception of incomplete objects or pictures. You may want to refer back to that section for these reasons. What the child remembers depends on what he has previously experienced. Thus, children vary greatly in what they remember, as a result of differences in experiences and subcultural membership (i.e., race, social class, rural-urban).

Level I. Prior to this level, the child's memory is dependent upon the continuation of his action toward or away from an object or event. At this level, memory appears as an internal representation of objects or events. Language (i.e., the naming of things) plays an important, although not exclusive part, in this development of memory as representation. This occurs when naming or labeling stimulates within the child's thinking meanings and images of absent objects or events. This causes them to be experienced by way of internal stimuli even though they are absent externally to the senses. Imitation and play, together with naming, stimulate memories at this level.

The child's memory for visual associations is increasing rapidly; this is evidenced by the child's gains in picture vocabulary. His visual memory for photographs of faces is present. The child can remember a simple visual cue for form or position for perhaps ten seconds; he shows this trait by finding a concealed toy that can only be located by using cues that have been associated previously with the toy. For instance, the object may be concealed in one of three shoe boxes, each of which is marked on top with a different small form (e.g., triangle, square, and circle). Motivation is usually high on such a task because the child wants to find the toy. Even when motivation is less apparent, as on a task which requires the child to place two simple forms in the same left-to-right order as was previously viewed in a picture model that is now out of view, the child may be able to complete the arrangement.

His development of memory in hearing, judging from his growth of vocabulary, is also increasing. The child can now retain a simple question or a command long enough to respond to it. The child repeats a three to four syllable statement (e.g., puppy dog eat) and on request repeats two to three numbers. The difference in favor of syllables over numbers occurs because meaning is present for the syllables and therefore aids memory. Immediate retention is better for meaningful material at all levels.

Level II. The child remembers for two or more seconds a picture that he has viewed briefly and can pick it from a set of pictures. He reliably selects from memory and correctly places two simple forms to match a picture display which is no longer visible.

The child's memory improves considerably for things which he hears. He repeats six to seven syllables of meaningful material and three numbers immediately after hearing them. He retains compound sentences for a period that is long enough for him to understand their meanings. Longer-term memory appears. For example, many children repeat four simple lines from memory, remember and recite some nursery rhymes, know parts or even the entirety of some songs, and interact in storytelling by filling in or identifying what they recall when they are questioned. (See the section on attention that describes the possible part which the child's preference for repetition, rehearsal, and the familiar plays in these gains.)

Level III. From memory, the child names which miniature, realistic object is missing from a small display which he studied prior to the secret removal of one of the objects. A clear progression is evident from level I through level III in this aspect of visual memory. Immediate recall for an arrangement of simple forms is increasing from two up to three objects for many children.

The child repeats a twelve syllable sentence of perhaps nine to ten words and repeats three to four numbers in correct sequence. He recites a poem and sings a song if he has had the opportunity to learn them.

Level IV. The child names pictured objects which have been removed from his sight. This is the first level at which visual memory for sequence is clearly present; the child reproduces from memory a three piece row of simple forms that is no longer visible to him. A few children correctly arrange four forms. His high level of success in the perception of incomplete objects implies that he has quite stable memory images.

He repeats four numbers and follows three instructions in proper order with only minor hesitations or mistakes; this shows that action is now directed in order by memory and that sequential memory is present for hearing as well as vision. He repeats a longer, more complicated sentence (e.g., I run to mother to ask for paper, pencil, and crayons.) Minor errors of singular and plural forms may occur in repetition of sentences. His memory structure is more integrated across sources of experience; therefore, the child is able to give a connected story of recent events.

Level V. The child's memory support or integration across different senses is now prominent; he improves his recall for new things which he experiences by naming or labeling out loud. His immediate visual memory for a sequence of simple forms is four.

The child immediately recalls four to five numbers; remembers his address, age, and possibly his date of birth; recites numbers to the thirties; and makes no mistakes in carrying out three instructions in proper order. After he has heard a story for the first time, he immediately recalls its main details. This kind of recall at level IV was only possible following a direct experience, but it now occurs through the hearing of a story. He recalls enough about stories to act them out in detail at a later time. The child's sequential memory in vision and hearing helps him to understand concepts that require a grasp of order (e.g., the concept of numbers as a sequence).

The child's span of immediate memory is approaching an upper limit; however, he may appear to have a larger memory span at a later date because the older child reintegrates what he sees or hears. The active processes or operations of memory are often referred to as memory strategies or information storage strategies, and the actual storage is referred to as memory proper. Such strategies of integrating information depend upon the availability of meanings and mediations. By the time he reaches level V, the child has become dependent upon meaning for immediate recall to the extent that he cannot remember a group of nonsense-ordered words (e.g., dog apple eat happy boy) as well as a child at level III or IV; however, he remembers a longer meaningful word group (i.e., a sentence) than children who are at a lower developmental level.

MEMORY OBJECTIVES FOR PRESCHOOL-AGED CHILDREN

1. To repeat simple nursery rhymes, poems, and songs that are used regularly at school.
2. To remember important personal data such as address and parents' names.
3. To recall the main details of stories, recite numbers in order, and follow at least three directions.

WHAT THE TEACHER DOES

There are many opportunities in an early childhood program to encourage children's memorization abilities. You can do this easily by teaching the children finger plays, rhymes, poems, and simple stories. Many times you can spontaneously initiate the finger play or song. For example, finding a spider might result in singing or saying "Itsy-Bitsy Spider." A sudden rain shower might suggest "Rain Is Falling Down" or "Rain, Rain Go Away." Songs, poems, and finger plays that are used in this way are enjoyable; the children do not think of them as lessons to be learned. There will be times in your program, though, when you will plan to teach specific songs or poems, but even then they should be taught in an enjoyable manner. Repetition through the use of records and tapes will also help them to learn more complex songs and stories.

A general strategy for you to follow is to spend time in discussion with the children. In these discussions, ask them what happened at breakfast or yesterday evening. Use their answers to probe further and to encourage them to recall details. Discuss what happened on last week's field trip. Structure your questions so that the children must recall details and cannot simply answer yes or no.

Another strategy is to ask questions which require the children to use labels that they are learning. For example, asking about shapes, colors, number of items, or names of animals or objects requires the child to recall information that he has used previously.

Help each child to learn his full name, his parents' names, and his phone number and address. You can provide opportunities in your program to let the child use these data. All of this practice is of course done orally for the young child. He can be encouraged to count and name the letters of the alphabet although you will want to be cautious that you are not simply encouraging repetition without any meaning attached to it.

Creative dramatics provides a means of fostering recall. After reading or telling a story to the children, ask them to act out parts of it. You can also ask them to tell you the main details or the sequence of events in the story. Children can demonstrate recall by acting out events which have taken place in their lives. The housekeeping and block building corners can be used to encourage this kind of activity. Of course, children must have varied experiences that are appropriate to act out in order to participate in a dramatic play. In some programs, you will want to provide many opportunities and experiences for the children through field trips and visits by resource persons to the center.

There are many games and manipulative activities which you can use to encourage memory. Asking the child to reproduce a simple block structure or a pattern with blocks requires him to use visual memory. Asking the child to recall what is missing from a tray of objects or around the room is another activity. Any time you change the room around or add something to it, ask the child about the changes; this activity requires the child to use his memory skills.

Concepts—Sequence of Developmental Behavior

The preconcepts that the child forms at levels I and II are very brief, and it is generally difficult to see how they relate to each other in any way; this is part of the reason why they are called *preconcepts* rather than *concepts*. At level III, the preconcepts become clearly interrelated so that the behaviors from which we judge the concepts to be present begin to fit into patterns. For levels IV and V, several separate, large concepts can be identified by name.

Level I. The child begins to form a preconcept that objects have names. He identifies persons and himself by name; this action shows that in his thinking they too are objects. He has a preconcept that a picture (symbol) can represent a real object. He understands the preconcept of possession (i.e., mine or my). He appears to understand adjectives for relative size (e.g., little, small, large), which implies a preconcept of size which is preliminary to number development. Although the child is only beginning to form a preconcept of number, he will pluralize by adding *s,* if he has picture supports; this shows a preliminary grasp of the distinction between *one* and *more than one* when identical objects are involved.

He begins to form an associative preconcept of function. When asked what he hears with, the child will point to his ears or name them. The preconcepts that children most often demonstrate when asked to describe objects are, in decreasing order of frequency, naming, class membership (e.g., a robin is called a bird instead of a robin), and function, with color mentioned by a few children. He does not yet complete simple, unfinished statements; he seems to lack preconcepts of associations or of completing a statement cooperatively. His construction of a tower of several cubes implies that he has a motor concept of space in which successive placements of blocks fill empty spaces (i.e., on top). His knowledge of location positions (i.e., on, under, in) implies at least an action oriented concept of position relative to other objects in space. His concept of causality is implied by a perception of persons or objects as sources of action.

Level II. Object and action naming is the most extensively used concept at this level. "What?" is the most frequent question. Color naming begins along with color matching, but it is quite limited. Objects retain their identities in miniature form and in picture representations, and pictures are now seen as suggesting action. Representational visual stimuli can signal for the child a wide variety of real objects and events. The concept of maleness/femaleness appears. The child's preconcept of possession expands to include others as well as oneself (i.e., his, hers). His preconcept of function or use is rapidly expanding, and it is perhaps the second most frequently used object concept at this level; it is demonstrated by both naming and pointing. In keeping with the preconcept of function, the child places doll furniture in appropriate groupings within rooms. He begins to see part/whole relationships as seen in his naming or pointing to parts of his own body and also to those of a doll. The child's questions about *where* suggest a preconcept of permanent location. He begins to complete a simple statement that was begun by someone else. Associative references to people or locations occur in the child's descriptions of objects. The child refers to some internal states (e.g., cold, sleepy, tired, hungry, thirsty); however, he refers to them in the present tense only. This suggests that they exist for the child only when the stimuli which produce them are actively experienced. By contrast, a primitive sense of past and present can be detected in the child's comprehension of language and occasionally in his expressive language. The child knows the preconcept of one in the context of eating, taking, or holding something.

Level III.   The child's tendency to name or label objects continues as strongly as at level II, but this tendency is now bypassed by the child's mention of function or use. Associations of objects to particular persons or contexts increase substantially in frequency. When requested to do so, the child will occasionally refer to the color and composition (i.e., metal, wood, cloth) of objects. If you ask him to tell about a picture, the child describes its parts by naming several of them. His naming of parts of a whole seems to parallel his thinking about part/whole relationships.

The child begins to assign similar things to classes (i.e., he sorts or groups). While naming may form a basis for grouping, the child most frequently groups on the basis of visual stimulus similarity (i.e., form, size, color, texture). At this level, the child understands the preconcept *alike* or *same*. Because the child's preconcept of identity has begun to move beyond that of single objects to the comparison of classes, he has acquired the foundations of correspondence of groups by matching them on a one-to-one basis perceptually. Both direct actions and visual impressions are used at this level to make groups of objects correspond, and the process is easily disturbed by questions or other incidental events. The child then becomes confused and cannot maintain the correspondence of groups.

The child counts to two or three. He can name the number of items in a group which contains two objects. His ability to compare the size of two objects (i.e., big/little, smaller/bigger) is increasing. At the same time, he begins to compare the weights of objects. He often comments on minor size differences. He uses the plural form for unfamiliar objects. All of these developments are the forerunners of the true concept of number in the child.

The child's knowledge of prepositions at this level implies a preconcept of action as well as location (e.g., up, down). This may mean that the preconcept of space is so flexible that the child can imagine not only locations but also movements within space. The increase of associations to context may suggest an increasingly internalized map of space which is constructed in part by the associations that exist between familiar objects and their customary locations.

The child's emerging preconcept of time may be seen in his use of language. He completes a sentence in the past tense (e.g., stopped), perfect tense (e.g., had stopped), and the continuing present tense (e.g., is crying). He also has a glimmering notion of one time of the day being earlier or later than another time. Things can happen *later* or *before*.

Up to this level, the child's sense of causality has depended on his own experience of bringing about change in his environment. His experience of desire has supported his belief in himself as a cause. In this connection, the child makes demands and gives commands. He has learned how to raise or lower the volume and rate of his speech; thus he gains further sense of control or causation over himself. By this level, if emotional development has progressed normally, he has learned that other people have desires and therefore operate in some manner as he does. This action may be signalled by the child asking questions which ask for the identity of the agent of some action. The child's development of causality at level III is shown by his use of the passive construction. He will comprehend and complete the sentence, "The door has been locked." The child thus behaves as if he accepts an unstated agent as the cause of the current condition of the door.

Level IV. The child forms true concepts at this level. It is easy to see how various groups of behavior fit together with reference to particular concepts. These concepts for which the behaviors were roughly grouped in level III can be examined from level IV onward in a more formal way as the concepts of object (naming and identity), classes or groups, number, space, time, causality, and nature.

Objects. The child describes objects in terms of functions, actions, or uses. He knows the function of the eyes, ears, legs, hands, and other obvious body parts. He makes associative references which relate objects to persons or places. The child is as likely to name or label objects, although he does this slightly less than at level III. The child's description of objects may include references to their color, shape, composition, important parts, and other physical characteristics. He will answer questions about the composition of objects, often knowing cloth, wood, leather, metal, and perhaps plastic. The child's adjectives describe the essential characteristics of objects (e.g., soft, happy, fast, pretty). His use of prepositional phrases describes the essential characteristics of objects (e.g., cup of coffee). He describes objects as belonging to people (e.g., Mary's hat). He recognizes all of the primary colors and can match them. Objects outside the child's immediate experience interest him, and he learns about them. He recognizes the age of persons, basing his impressions mainly on physical size. Many of the properties of objects which the child identifies at level IV will eventually permit him to group objects more abstractly at level V (e.g., by function or composition). He asks the meanings of words in an effort to understand objects.

Classes.   Part/whole relationships are becoming firmly established; the child finishes incomplete sentences (e.g., Our hands have ———.). The child puts similar or identical objects in classes. He applies adjectives to classes of objects as well as to individual objects. The child sorts a set of objects for both color and form at the same time (bidimensional sorting). He completes simple "opposite analogies," picks out the one that does not belong or is not the same, identifies pictorial likenesses and differences, and goes through a set of objects labeling each one as *different* or the *same* as compared to some standard concept.

Number.   When the child is given a group of sticks or rods of varying lengths and asked to put them in order from small to large ("make these go up like stairs"), he almost always correctly compares two sticks; but he cannot coordinate the series beyond a comparison of individual pairs. Therefore, his final arrangement appears to be a jumble of unrelated pairs which have been placed next to each other. This relates to classes by showing that the child only vaguely comprehends what a series of little to big might be; therefore, he arranges individual parts according to this size relationship but cannot arrange the whole by using the same principle. He compares relative amounts such as more/less, heavy/light, higher/lower, and faster/slower. He can reliably count four or five objects. If he is shown three objects, he immediately responds that he sees three and seems to have a firm grasp of this number. However, beyond five objects, his counting is unstable. He will sometimes skip an object when counting, count the same object twice, or leave out a number. Counting seems to be an imitative action based on the child's memory of adult counting behavior. He stacks correctly a tower of five graduated size blocks; he shows some capacity to arrange objects in an order when the number of objects is small and the stimulus supports are strong. Blocks provide more perceptual cues for ordering than sticks. Apparently, the growing strength of the child's top-to-bottom scanning visual habit accounts for the greater difficulty of making a horizontal arrangement.

Space.   The child understands that containers hold liquid and that a container can be empty, full, or partially filled. The child understands that people live in homes and go to other places to work. He has a relative concept of distance (i.e., far, near) which is added to his sense of location (i.e., by, between, in front of).

Time. The child distinguishes morning from night. His comprehension of these times relates mainly to his experiences of what happens at night (e.g., parent comes home; he eats supper, sleeps) and morning (e.g., wakes up, eats breakfast, parent goes to work). He understands the concepts *early* and *late*. He uses the future tense in addition to the past and present tense. Questions of *when* become more prominent in his speech.

Causality. The questions of *why* and *how* become quite noticeable at this level; this suggests that the child is seeking information about causes and the processes by which things happen. He understands simple cause-effect relationships.

Nature. This category is reserved for events in nature which are not described under the other categories. If you are interested in preschool science, you will want to examine the entire section on concepts. The child is familiar with the basic features of the weather (e.g., cool, clouds, rain, fog, possibly snow, ice, wind, etc.).

Level V. The child continues his progress in the development of true concepts. The organization of these major concepts becomes increasingly clear.

Objects. Further changes are seen in the child's descriptions of objects. He still most often groups objects together by their function; however, when he defines words, his references to function decrease. Similarly, he identifies which things act in certain ways (e.g., skate, swim, climb trees). Associational references to persons or places follow the functional references in importance. These types of descriptions are followed, in decreasing order of usage, by references to shape (which increases greatly), naming (which continues to decrease), important parts (which has greatly increased), color (increases), composition (increases), other physical characteristics (increases), comparison (increases), and number reference (increases). All of these increases account for a much more complete object description than at level IV. Some physical qualities which were previously used only for the sense of touch are used for hearing (e.g., soft). Individual pictured forms are matched for identity (just alike) and for similarity (almost alike). The child's identity and similarity matching skills are less developed for grouping objects according to size. The child is aware of a person's age on the basis of facial cues in addition to size, and he knows his own age. He can transform actions (verbs) into objects (nouns) (e.g., drive into driver). The child asks for the meanings of words as he did at level IV; however, he now asks for meanings with abstract characteristics. This last change suggests that his developing concept of objects is gradually leading to an awareness of complex, abstract ideas.

With the guidance of the teacher, children examine a bug that was discovered in the school yard.

Classes. The child tells how two familiar objects are alike and different; specifies how two dissimilar or two familiar objects might be used; explains how things differ; uses antonyms, synonyms, opposite analogies, and contrasts more freely; recognizes words that have opposite and like meanings; verbally assigns objects to classes; completes opposite analogies requiring different grammatical forms (noun, verb, or adjective); and points to what is different or alike. These behaviors show a capacity to verbally classify or group objects. Before this level, *same* and *different* referred to perceptual/motor processes, but now they are also related to processes.

Number. The child uses the correct singular/plural forms for nouns (e.g., man/men) but not for irregular verbs (e.g., is/are). His number related language has increased greatly (e.g., large, small, some, not many, longest, shortest, few, widest, largest, smallest, tallest, most, whole, every, not any more, several, as many, not first, and last).

He counts to twelve or more; and within the range of his correct counting, he can tell what number follows another number. When he counts beyond twelve, he skips or repeats numbers. He matches two sets of moveable objects according to number when the number of elements in the sets does not exceed ten. If he has to equate two sets of pictures of objects, he may not correctly count the objects. He cannot count in reverse.

He knows that cutting something in half leaves two pieces. He comprehends the concepts of one-third and one-fourth. He divides an area in half and again into quarters by visual estimation, but he cannot explain his action, and he cannot divide an area into thirds. He cannot comprehend units that measure length.

The child builds a tower of five graduated blocks more quickly than he did at level IV. He knows first, middle, last, and possibly second; some children know the concepts of fourth and medium-sized. He can discriminate size differences of sticks easier than he can arrange them into a series; the child has as much difficulty counting them as arranging them. The child arranges most of the sticks in order, with some mix-ups; he can correct these mistakes by trial and error. His behavior suggests that he uses a perceptual image of the series and that this image can only guide him in matching behaviors but cannot provide him with a strategy for ordering the full series. By this level, many children can do a very simple addition and subtraction of concrete objects.

Space. The left-right convention appears at this level, usually following intentional instruction. This convention implies an ordering of oneself and later of space with reference to the sides of one's body. The child's vocabulary for spatial relations includes words like top, through, inside, middle, next to, farthest, around, over, between, nearest, corner, row, center, side, below, forward, above, in order, behind, separated.

When the child is asked to match drawings of identical objects which have been rotated into different positions in space, his skill is far behind that for form identity and similarity matching. This skill of dealing with spatial rotations has only begun to develop at this level.

The spatial concept of a distance between two points is disturbed at this level if a barrier is placed between the two end points. Apparently, the child cannot coordinate his understanding of the two parts created by the barrier with his understanding of the whole distance. If a straight string and a wavy string have end points which fall next to each other, only some children will recognize that one piece of string is longer than the other; when the wavy string is straightened out to its full length, more (but not all) of the children will recognize that the lengths are different. The child seems to center his attention upon the end points when he estimates the distance between two points. If two equally long rods are placed side by side and then if one is moved slightly ahead of the other, the child no longer sees the two rods as being the same length. Therefore, the child becomes confused when he tries to compare distances particularly when the starting points are different or irregular routes are taken. In contrast, the child can comprehend the equivalence or disequality between two areas. For example, if the child sees a picture of two fields which have the same area and if cattle are added to one field, he will still see both fields as being equivalent in area. On the other hand, if a house is added to one of the fields, he will see that the field with the house on it now has less vacant space than the other field. The basis of this judgment is still the child's perception rather than his understanding of the constancy of area.

Time.   The child can distinguish between morning and afternoon. The child correctly forms the perfect tense with the auxiliary verb (e.g., had stopped, have seen); nonstandard English usage may obscure this fact with some children.

Causality.   The child uses the passive form of verbs more consistently and with variations in verb tenses (e.g., cake was eaten). He sees other persons as sources of favors and expresses his appreciation or gratitude; they are hence causes. He seems to have a limited view of social causality in that he judges that adults act only from benevolence or kindness rather than from duty or self-interest. He begins to attribute motives and intentions to others. He begins to develop a notion of physical causality that is separate from his feelings.

Nature.   The child recognizes topographical features within the range of his own experience or what he has learned through stories. He may recognize oceans, lakes, rivers, mountains, valleys, woods, etc. For each of these features, he can mention or describe a prominent identifying characteristic (e.g., a mountain is *high, pointed*).

CONCEPT OBJECTIVES FOR PRESCHOOL-AGED CHILDREN

Objects

1.   To give more complete descriptions of the qualities of objects.
2.   To show a growing awareness of abstract ideas (e.g., sweet, older, prettier, easy).

Classes

1. To verbally classify things according to whether they are the same or different (e.g., they look alike or they do not look alike; they sound alike or they do not sound alike).
2. To group things which go together.

Number

1. To arrange on the basis of verbal instruction, objects of varying lengths from small to large so that they match a visible model.
2. To arrange three objects of varying sizes in order from small to large.
3. To tell which of two objects is larger or smaller.
4. To tell which of two areas is larger or smaller.
5. To acquire a vocabulary of number related words.
6. To count accurately. (See individual levels for counting expectations.)
7. To know the ordinal positions of first, middle, and last.
8. To understand that something that is cut into halves leaves two pieces.

Space

1. To acquire a receptive vocabulary for spatial relationships (e.g., top, middle, corner).
2. To develop a concept of distance (e.g., far, near).
3. To indicate the relative positions of things to one's body (e.g., behind, in front of, inside, outside).
4. To extend the concept of relative position from oneself to other objects (e.g., next to the table).

Time

1. To relate the times of the day to activities that take place during the day.
2. To use the future tense, present perfect tense, and past perfect tense in addition to the present and past tenses.
3. To recognize before, after, later.

Causality

1. To seek information about cause-effect relationships.

2. To experience himself as a cause of things that happen in his environment.

3. To experience outside objects and things as causes and effects and to eventually understand that only animate things cause effects.

Nature

1. To recognize major land features and weather phenomena that are within the realm of the child's experience.

WHAT THE TEACHER DOES

To sharpen the child's observations about how things are alike and different, how things are arranged or ordered, and why things happen, you should provide a wide variety of experiences and materials with which the child can interact; this will also provide you with the opportunity to raise questions and call attention to certain phenomena. If children are to have the opportunity to develop the concepts of which they are capable, they must be provided with a rich and thought-provoking environment. It must also be a changing environment if it is to provide for the changing interests and abilities of the children. In a thought-provoking environment the children will develop concepts more readily when concept related features of the environment are discussed and drawn to their attention.

Experiences which contribute greatly to concept development usually fall within the realm of the sciences, social studies, mathematics, and literature. Although the child develops concepts in relation to experiences in art, music, and language arts, he mainly uses these areas to express concepts that are in the process of development. In other words, you may obtain evidence of the child's concept development through what he talks about and how he talks about it or what he paints and how he goes about painting. Experiences in the expressive arts are very important, but they cannot take the place of experiences which provide the bulk of the information which the child must acquire and process.

The child acquires some concepts through the use of materials such as blocks, puzzles, letters, games, sand, and water. You may use many materials and experiences for concept development when the opportunity arises or when their use is acceptable to the child, but you must plan experiences to make sure that the opportunity does arise. You also have to make some decisions regarding the kind of situation in which you can best teach a concept. For example, if you are trying to teach a concept of shape, it is more appropriate to give a child different shapes to manipulate on a flannel board or to sort than to try to teach the concept during an art activity. In the first activity, you can concentrate on separating the triangles, circles, and squares on the board whereas in the art activity, you may reduce the child's interest in the art activity if you do more than mention that some of the shapes are triangles, circles, etc.

Use your observations to help in deciding what concepts the children are able to learn or what ones will be interesting to them, and plan opportunities for these learning experiences. This section of the text should be helpful in providing ideas, although the examples are necessarily limited. There are many textbooks and guides which provide additional examples; and local, state, and national professional groups provide workshops which may furnish you with ideas. The experiences which help to develop perception are also helpful in this area.

Objects.   The list of experiences which might be used to promote object description is almost endless. The more realistic the examples are, the better. Many of the experiences fall within the area of science—observing and describing the characteristics of hamsters, puppies, kittens, birds, earthworms, frogs, fish, turtles; plant life such as seasonal changes in trees, flowers, and seeds; inanimate objects such as stones, wood, plastic, rubber, glass. For example, the preceding list can be described in terms of furry, soft, hard, sharp, shiny, etc. Cooking can be an especially valuable activity because of the variety of foods which may be used and because of the physical and chemical changes which occur in the food. Most experiences can be provided on an informal basis (i.e., they can be brought into the classroom, and the children can watch or participate if they are interested). It is usually neither necessary nor desirable to have the whole class participate at the same time in an activity because this results in much unnecessary waiting. Four or five children can usually have a satisfying cooking experience at one time. An experience such as cooking can be repeated with another group either that day or the next day. All children can have an opportunity to observe a frog or a rabbit at some time during a day, and the animal might remain in the classroom for several days or until the children seem to have gained the major learning experiences that it can provide.

You do far more than provide the experience. The experience is simply the "raw material." You should try to give some focus to what the children can do with the experience. What is it? and What does it do? These questions can be asked by you or the children. The youngest children may not go beyond these questions, but the more advanced children can be asked questions such as, What color is it? What is its shape? How does it feel? Encourage the children to use as many descriptive words as possible, and supply some of your knowledge to supplement what the children already know. Do not expect every child to be able to answer all of the questions that you may ask. Repeated opportunities should be provided for the children to handle and experiment with objects that will facilitate the development of concepts and require the use of descriptive language. Children build new concepts on the background they already have, so repetition of similar experiences after a lapse of time may also be beneficial.

Classes.   The early classification experiences usually consist of simple sorting exercises. If you give the child an assorted box of colored beads, he can be asked to pick out the red ones, the ones with square sides, the large ones, etc. Children can stack all of the blocks that are the same size in one space on a shelf. Many materials that may be sorted are available at little or no cost (e.g., boxes of buttons, spools, medium and large nails, medium and large bolts, etc.).

Create activities which fit the child's abilities. In the beginning, the similarity and difference between objects should be very noticeable so the classifications can be made easily if the child knows the concept of sameness. As your children understand the idea of classification, they can learn to classify objects that float or sink, objects that are picked up or not picked up by a magnet, etc. Cooking experiences offer many opportunities for classification—some ingredients are liquid, some are solid, some are powdered; some foods are vegetables, some are fruits, some are desserts, some are meats. Children respond well to the occasional use of such statements as "all the children who are wearing red may go to get their coats" or "all the children who are wearing black shoes may go to the table now." With the children who are at levels IV and V, you can use games which encourage matching and classification. The simplest ones are lotto games which require the child to match a picture on a small card to an identical picture on a card containing several pictures. Lotto games are easy when the pictures are simple and easily distinguishable but become more difficult if the pictures are very similar. You can create games by mounting pictures of objects that serve similar functions on cards and having the children select the ones that go together. Another type of game requires the sorting of items that go together such as those which are found in a grocery store, in a dress shop, in a barber shop, etc.

Number. Classroom experiences that require the use of numerical concepts are more interesting to children than direct attempts at teaching specific concepts. Materials such as graduated blocks and sticks, a change carrier, cash register, rulers, measuring spoons, cups and measuring containers, play money, scales, large paper or plastic numerals, counting books, and books about number concepts are all helpful in the development of numerical concepts. These are materials which can be incorporated into children's play and which permit you to talk with the children about number and quantity. As children play with blocks, you can use the terms "large" or "small," etc.

Develop an awareness of numerical language in the children. For example, as children engage in carpentry, refer to the longer or shorter piece of wood, the larger or smaller nail, the narrow or wide board. In a cooking experience, you have terms such as teaspoon, tablespoon, cup; you use fractions such as one-fourth and one-half. When it is necessary to take turns, refer to who is first, second, third, last, etc. In art activities, refer to the large chalk, the small brush, etc. This use of number related language in a context in which it can be understood is very important.

Use daily experiences to develop an awareness of numbers in the children. For example, cups, napkins, pieces of paper, children, and other things may be counted from time to time. Let the children help or do the counting as they become more competent. Let them help to divide materials such as large pieces of paper that need to be divided. As the paper is divided say, "Here is half for Jimmy and half for Sue," or "We'll fold the paper in half and then you can cut down the line."

Use your ingenuity in initiating activities such as weighing or measuring objects in the room. The children are the most obvious objects for weighing. You can also weigh dolls, a toy truck, a plant, a pet, or other objects that the children suggest. A neat trick is to give the child something to hold while he is on the scale so that he can see what happens. Take the children to the grocery or drug store to buy an object for the classroom. Use an old telephone so that the children can practice dialing their own telephone numbers. Sit at a small table with two or three of the more advanced children and devise number games which involve counting, matching, and simple addition and subtraction of objects. For example, give each child eight toy horses to count. Then give them toy men which they would first count and later match to the horses. Then add horses or men or remove some of the horses or men and discuss whether you have more or less horses or men. Continue this kind of activity only as long as the children are interested, and adjust the activity to the abilities of the children.

Space. Everyday activities provide many opportunities for the exploration and understanding of spatial relationships as well as for the aquisition of the vocabulary that goes with the experiences. On the climber, a child can be "above" all the other children, "below" another child, or "beside" another child. When riding a tricycle, the child always has the problem of determining how much space he needs to pass or to turn the corner without getting off the hard-surfaced area. Block building is an especially good activity for exploring the concepts of vertical and horizontal space. In connection with the objects that children build with blocks, you can use terms such as "through" the tunnel, "over" the bridge, "around" the curve, "inside" the garage, etc; in this way, you give the children the words to describe the concepts that are shown in his constructions. When the children put toys away, indicate whether they go "on top of" the cabinet, on the "middle" shelf, or in the "bottom" drawer. Pass cookies to the child "next" to you, ask Horatio to sit in the chair "between" Jack and Angela, or place the flowers in the "center" of the table. Tell Lena to look "behind" her for the ball, to hold the book "in front of" her, or to hold the thimble "inside" both hands. If the child does not comprehend the concept, you will need to demonstrate or explain it to him.

Frequently, children's activities must be regulated in terms of distance. If a play area lacks a fence or if not all of the play area is to be used, you might say, "Stay on this side of the big tree," or "Go as far as the hedge, then come back." If the class is out for a walk, you might say, "Wait for me at the end of the block," "Our walk will be three blocks long," or "We are taking a bus today because it is too far to walk to the dairy." A child may also talk about a child who lives "near" him or about traveling "far, far" away on an airplane to visit grandmother.

Time. Explanations are often necessary to help children understand the concept of time. Five minutes can be a long or short period of time depending on whether the child is interested in something or is waiting for you to finish the story that you are writing for Jimmy. You can clarify the meaning of time by speaking of the sequence in which activities will occur (e.g., "We will go outside after our story." "First wash your hands and then we will eat the pieces of apple." "Monday is the first day of the week that we go to school." "The music teacher comes on Friday.")

Although children cannot tell time at this age, they are interested in the clock and like to be shown what the clock looks like when some of their favorite activities take place. Older preschool children respond well to statements such as "It will be lunchtime when the clock looks like this," and they will watch a clock to see when the time comes.

Preschool children should not be told too far in advance of approaching events because the time seems so long for them. Also, as the time draws nearer, the certainty that the event will occur is greater, lessening the possibility of disappointment. It is best not to inform preschool children of plans for a trip until two or three days in advance. Most teachers also advise against a long preparation for holidays because of the excitement which builds up within the child.

Causality. Because causality in preschool-aged children is so inadequately understood, you should be more concerned with creating an interest in cause and effect than with an actual understanding of causality. Many experiences which were mentioned in previous sections of the text on concepts can be used to encourage the asking of *why* and *how* questions. Although you may give the child a logical explanation in response to his question, do not assume that he understands the answer.

Children often ask questions which require very complex answers. In dealing with such questions it is sometimes helpful to respond with a "What do you think?" question instead of immediately giving an answer. This enables you to learn more about the child's thoughts before you give an explanation. Often the child enjoys talking about what he thinks. You do not have to provide all of the information you know to answer a preschooler's question. Give a simple, but factual, answer and leave the child free to ask another question. Also, be careful in handling the child's misconceptions; permit him to feel good about what he knows rather than trying to correct all of his mistakes. Sometimes you may be able to provide an experience which will help correct the misconception, but sometimes you should simply listen and say nothing. As the child's thinking abilities become more advanced, his concepts will change.

Children can be made aware of some simple cause-effect situations in the classroom. You may stand dominoes on end so that when you touch the first one, it will knock down the next one and so on until the whole stack falls. Show the child that the teeter-totter flies up when he gets off or show him how to pump in the swing so that he can experience himself as a cause. Also, show him how he can do things like making green from mixing yellow and blue or how he can make the clay or dough too sticky by using too much water. In social situations, children must learn that when they hit other children, they get mad and hit back.

Nature. Involve children in activities which will help them to learn about weather and land features of the area in which they live. Engage them in discussions about whether the day is sunny, cloudy, rainy, snowy; whether it is hot, cool, warm; whether the weather will permit them to go outdoors; and whether they will need wraps, mittens, or boots.

Usually, children talk about land features in their discussions on the places where they live and the places where they visit either with their families or in school. A class may take a walk in the woods or go for a boat ride on a lake. Their school may be located at the top of a hill, or a river may flow through the town. Often, stories include references to land features that may need explanation or encourage discussion. Your encouragement can often lead children into elaborate descriptions of their experiences with lakes, mountains, or the ocean.

The teaching problem associated with this category is an endless repetition of the same experiences. Be sure that you are actually extending the child's concepts, not just repeating over and over again information that he already knows. Many science experiences can be the outgrowth of the child's interest in weather or land features. This interest also leads to play activities such as making rivers and lakes in the sandbox and pretending to ride in a boat that is made of blocks.

Language—Sequence of Developmental Behavior

Level I. The child comprehends 200 to 300 words. His picture vocabulary is growing rapidly for familiar objects (nouns) and actions (verbs). He inhibits to the command, "No, no." He may recognize one or two prepositions, probably including *on.* He follows simple commands when materials are in plain view, answers simple questions, obeys simple directions, points to smaller parts of his body when requested to do so, comprehends the words for close family relationships, and points to objects which are identified by their uses. His comprehension is adequate for a familiar speaker who can adapt vocabulary and sentence construction to the child's understanding.

By gesture, he conveys his understanding of the uses of one or two common household objects. His expressive vocabulary may consist of 50 words. He names pictures of familiar objects; names the obvious body parts of himself or a doll; says his name; and uses *mine, me, you,* and *I,* in this order of appearance (and frequently correctly). Typically, he forms a two to three word sentence; tells when he needs to go to the toilet or asks for help; talks aloud to himself; asks the names of some objects; talks about pictures that are shown to him; requests *more* or *another;* pluralizes words by adding *s* or *es;* tells what to do with pencil, knife, ball, shoe; tells about his desire to eat or drink. He may talk about what he is doing while doing it; however, he usually leaves out the articles (a, an, the). He may use the past tense although he mainly uses the active present verb tense. Gestures, grunts, and tugging at an adult may substitute for what he lacks in expressive language. This is called the early sentence stage and is marked by the child's heavy use of nouns and his lack of articles and auxiliary verbs; also, he uses few prepositions or conjunctions. About 40 percent of the child's sentences are *functional sentences* (i.e., complete sentences that are incorrect grammatically); 30 percent are *simple sentences* (i.e., sentences that are grammatically complete with a noun and verb); and 8 percent are *elaborated sentences* (i.e., sentences that contain prepositional phrases and compound or complex sentences).

The child prominently displays imitative and repetitive motor behavior, i.e., the child repeats words or sounds. He attempts to join an adult in songs or creates a phrase of his own, but the effect is not musical. He often repeats himself.

Level II. The child points to identify more pictures than he formerly identified (including less frequently used words like *teacher, sewing,* and *arrow*); comprehends most common verbs; comprehends many common adjectives; comprehends more prepositions; acts or stops his behavior to a one word command (e.g., "No" or "Stop"); and knows the labels for the less commonly named body parts (e.g., *teeth, chin*). He understands longer, more complex sentences; carries out three simple instructions in order; and listens to a story that he knows. He does not tire of the same picture book story. There are no reliable estimates of the child's total receptive vocabulary for levels II through V, although it apparently increases enormously during these years.

The child uses expressive gestures more extensively than he did at level I, but they still deal with essentially the same things. His expressive vocabulary consists of 200 or more words, but his speech is still immature. He now says his full name; refers to himself in speech with the appropriate pronoun; names nearly all common pictures; uses the correct verb forms to identify simple actions that are shown in pictures; names one color; uses the articles more regularly; uses *his, hers,* and other personal pronouns. He can correctly refer to persons (1st, 2nd, or 3rd) but may use the wrong case (i.e., *he, him,* or *his*). Typically, his sentences consist of three to four words, of which 35 percent are functional types, 42 percent are simple, and 10 percent are elaborated. He recites four lines from memory; relates what has just occurred; tells what he is about to do; expresses upset emotions over the mistakes of others; verbalizes his desire to do what someone else is doing; describes his drawings; asks, What? and may occasionally ask, Why? How? or Where?; tells what he does when he feels tired, hungry, or cold although he may give a very personal reaction (e.g., "I not tired."); uses some plural forms correctly; increases his use of the negative command from *no* to *don't*; gives irrelevant answers when questions become too difficult (e.g., when asked what flies, he might answer "House."); talks about contemporary events during his play; and stutters when he is excited. He gives some associational responses to questions (e.g., When asked what eats, he might reply, "Table eats.")

The child imitates and practices language through syntactic play; for example, he arranges and rearranges word orders, transforms sentences and substitutes words in fixed sentence locations. What may appear to the adult to be repetitious talk may in fact be serious language practice. The child repeats a six to seven syllable sentence.

Level III. The child usually comprehends sentences in context quite well. He has difficulty comprehending isolated words out of context. He comprehends in context adverbs of spatial position or direction (e.g., up, down), adjectives, more prepositions, and most common nouns and verbs. It is easier for the child to identify a word from pictures because picture vocabulary provides some context clues while words that are isolated from context do not. The child's

picture vocabulary increases substantially during this level and begins to include more abstract and uncommon nouns and nouns
which must be distinguished from other members of the same class
(e.g., he must choose an automobile from among other means of
transportation). The child comprehends comparative statements in
a visual context, compound sentences, and *why* questions; follows
directions to perform more than one action; and comprehends noun
phrases that contain two adjective modifiers.

His gestural pantomime skills increase, but he uses them mainly
to show how to use simple articles for grooming or the most common
household articles. The child names most colors; volunteers four or
more prepositions in response to stimulus pictures (may use new
words such as *on top of, under, inside*); uses adverbs and adjectives
and most common nouns and verbs; refers to himself by pronoun;
completes opposite analogies; names his own drawing; and displays
an expressive vocabulary of perhaps 1,200 words. Among his most
frequently used words are *I, it, you, that, a, do, this, not, the.* The
child names many animals and begins to supply the class names for
groups of things (e.g., numbers, chairs).

He can complete sentences in the passive voice and the progressive
present tense. He can relate what has just happened, recite a nursery rhyme, remember the words of a song, name three or more
objects when he is asked to tell about a picture, add phrases to simple
predications (e.g. adds the phrase *to the store* to *I run*), ask many
questions, give two or more responses to a question if the listener
keeps waiting, and form five-word sentences. He makes few paragraph length expressions. He correctly responds to *why* questions,
whispers, controls the speed and loudness of his speech, talks to
himself about what is happening, begins to ask *who* questions, describes an object from a picture, and spontaneously shares experiences and describes activities. The child demands, commands, and
negates statements.

He forms sentences which are slightly longer and less like those
of the preceding level. His statements are less like motor actions and
are more cognitive to the degree that they refer to happenings in the
distant past or those which have a future intent. Functional sentences comprise 32 percent of his total speech; simple sentences, 38
percent; and elaborated sentences, 17 percent. Only one or two sentences out of 50 are compound or complex. The subject-predicate and
object of verb forms are distinct in his speech. Frequently, the child
forms the incorrect past tense for irregular verbs because he tries to
apply the same rules to irregular verbs that he applies to regular

verbs (e.g. he will form the past tense of put by adding *ed*); he makes the same kind of error when he forms the plural of irregular nouns (e.g., he will add *s* to man to form the plural). He can repeat six- and seven-word sentences when he is requested to do so.

Level IV. The child comprehends the words *by, between, in front of.* He understands most common pronouns (gender and number) but still confuses *he* and *she* with *they.* He uses prepositions (e.g., the word "behind") to guide his actions toward or away from some location. He follows or "reads" a story from pictures and recognizes its main theme. He comprehends simple and compound directions to act. He identifies and picks out a picture which has been described to him. The child pantomimes the behavior of others. He uses perhaps 1,500 words; prints simple words; uses pronouns about as well as he comprehends them; and uses verbs in the future tense. His picture vocabulary grows to include less familiar words that are drawn from outside the child's immediate environment.

This is the complete sentence stage; the child typically forms sentences of five or six words, and he often forms sentences with seven and eight words. The greater complexity of the child's sentences is apparent from his use of relative pronouns (i.e., which, of, that) and fairly correct formation of endings for nouns and verbs. Functional sentences account for 32 percent of his sentences; simple, 32 percent; and elaborated, 21 percent. Compound and complex sentences are becoming more common in his speech. The child's conversations approach paragraph length. The child classifies or categorizes verbally and formally defines the names of objects, using description or category placement or usage. He begins to respond appropriately to simple questions and gives focused answers that are often unlike the associative answers of levels II and III. He tells a story about a picture and repeats a familiar story. The child interprets simple abstractions (e.g., the meaning of *brave*); expresses ideas based on his personal experience; shares information and impressions; tells a complete version of something that he has seen or experienced, says where he lives and may give his age. He continues to ask many questions (many fall into the *how, why,* and *when* categories); completes simple analogies about uses or actions; listens to and repeats long stories; talks to himself and others; confuses fact and fantasy; and sensibly answers *why* questions. In terms of difficulty, the most to least difficult sentence types for him to understand are as follows: negative, passive, question, and active.

The child repeats an eight-word sentence containing a preposi-tional phrase (e.g., *on the fence*), an adverbial clause (e.g., *before I could tell him*), or a complicated verbal form (e.g., *to go to the store; helping my mother*).

Level V.   The child understands only a few adjectives of number or relative quantity (e.g., *first*); knows more difficult nouns which are formed from verbs (e.g., *swimmer* and *swimming* from *swim*); and recognizes pictures that show objects that are not part of his experi-ence (e.g., tractor, traffic signal). He understands passive sentences better than negative ones, although the opposite appears to be true for his formation of sentences; responds with humor to silly or ab-surd statements; likes to hear riddles; and understands the contrast between singular nouns and plural nouns for classes of things but does not fully understand the same contrasts for the verb form *is* and *are*.

The child's nonverbal expression through pantomime continues to expand for identifying objects which he has only observed adults use. He appropriately names pictures which depict nouns, pronouns, verbs, and prepositions; names a penny, nickel, and a dime; recites numbers to thirty; prints his name and copies familiar words; uses the auxiliary verb *have* and the past tense; increases his use of adjectives and adverbs; nominalizes (i.e., forms nouns from verbs); freely uses synonyms and antonyms; and has an expressive vocabu-lary of over 2,000 words.

The child tells original, fanciful stories in language that is essen-tially complete in structure. His sentences are typically six to seven words long. About 32 percent of his sentences are of the functional type; 29 percent, simple; and 23 percent, elaborated. When telling about pictures, he goes beyond the immediately available informa-tion to make inferences. He expresses appreciation, tells where he lives if he did not do this at level IV, and asks the meanings of abstract words; he defines nouns by their use if asked to do so, but if asked only to define, he is less likely to refer to use than he did formerly. He answers questions sensibly; defines more words; regu-larly uses the correct forms for the third person present or past tense of verbs (e.g., she *goes*/ she *went*); more regularly uses prepositions and articles; makes fewer mistakes when he forms the plural forms of irregular verbs and nouns; and correctly uses the perfect tenses. He repeats sentences of nine or more words when he is requested to do so.

LANGUAGE OBJECTIVES FOR
PRESCHOOL-AGED CHILDREN

1. To understand and use active and question sentences and increasingly to understand negative sentences and use passive sentences.

2. To use sentences that consist of six to seven words.

3. To increase in his ability to use the language forms of the adults around him.

4. To have the language structure and vocabulary to tell original stories.

5. To become increasingly able to pantomime experiences that he has had plus the experiences that he has observed in others.

6. To show an interest in the meaning of new and abstract words.

WHAT THE TEACHER DOES

Language development is a basic component of the early childhood program. You will want to insure that each child has an ample opportunity to practice his language. Since language development is closely connected to concept development, memory, mediation, and some aspects of perception at these levels, encourage the children to verbalize as they learn and play. They should talk out loud, for example, as they manipulate objects, build with blocks, and construct with art media or construction equipment. If you respond to their talk at the appropriate times, you can often encourage further verbalization on the part of the children. Often just saying, "Oh yes" or "Really" indicates to the children that you are listening to them and will encourage them to continue talking. The alert teacher helps children to express their ideas by providing words for which they are groping or by providing the sentence structure that they are unable to produce. An example of this problem would be the child who is trying to tell you that he has four pet turtles at his house but can only relate this idea to you by counting. He might say, "I have my turtle, and the big turtle, and Tommy's turtle, and another little turtle." You can pull everything together for him and say, "Then you have four turtles at your house. Is that right?"

The young child learns his language from the adults around him; therefore, his language skills can only be as complete as the models he hears. Since the child can comprehend more than he can actually produce, do not always simplify what you say to him. Although it is often necessary to give directions in short sentences, use natural conversational patterns when you are discussing ideas, pictures, stories, or trips.

Use records, tapes, television, films, and filmstrips to provide a wide variety of voices, topics, dialects, and language experiences for the children. Resources can add to the child's vocabulary along with presenting new ideas.

There are many language stimulation games that you can use with the children. Almost any game which requires the player to label or name adds to the child's vocabulary; lotto games are especially good. Verbal games such as "Riddle Riddle Ree, I See Something You Don't See" are good for language development. Sometimes you will have to lead the activity and help to keep it simple enough for the children at this level. Games and activities that require describing are useful since children are really learning how to use adjectives in the preschool years. For example, the Sesame Street game, "One of These Things Is Not Like the Other" requires the child to describe why one picture or object is different from the others. Describing pictures, especially with a group of children, increases vocabulary.

Structure activities and games that require the child to act out prepositions such as *in, out, through, by.* (Note that games, in this context, are very unstructured and informal). For example, playing an "over" and "under" game on the playground equipment helps the children to understand the use of these prepositions. Later, you can relate prepositions to paper and pencil tasks, puzzles, forms, etc. There are several good picture books for children that are particularly helpful with these concepts and grammatical constructions.

Expose your children to a wide range of ideas and language by reading many stories to them. For variety, use flannel board stories, story cards, and storytelling. The many ideas and language styles that children acquire from stories and books provide a wide array of language models for the child. Stories stimulate discussion and conversation among the children. Children at the upper levels can tell stories from the pictures in their picture books. Encourage them to "read" to each other in this way; this fosters the idea that one can get information and enjoyment from printed material.

Puppet activities encourage the verbalization and retelling of stories. An elaborate puppet theater and set of puppets are not necessary. Make a theater from a large box. Children can make puppets from milk cartons, paper cups, scrap materials, papier-mâché, or paper bags. Playing with puppets stimulates conversation, and the actual making of the puppets also stimulates oral language.

Keep a variety of dress-up outfits in the room for spontaneous dramatic play. A box of scarves or hats can serve this purpose. Stay with the children when the occasion demands it to help them verbalize their ideas and feelings.

You should begin to use story dictation in the preschool years. As the children tell you about their art work, print their sentences for them. In the earliest stages, it is sufficient to label their art work. Eventually, they will want to dictate stories about pictures that they are viewing or experiences that they have had. They may or may not want to illustrate their stories. By the time children reach higher levels, they can dictate notes to sick classmates, to their parents about school activities, or for greeting cards.

Activities should be planned which help the children to raise and answer questions. For example, the germination of seeds helps the children to see relationships between the seed, the plant, and the fruit, flower, or vegetable. Complex sentences which include if-when clauses, conjunctions, and cause and effect relationships become necessary to adequately describe or explain what is happening. The child at all levels is developing these sentence forms. He will need your help to express his ideas using these forms. You should discuss reasons for events in the child's life to help him see cause and effect relationships. Small group discussions are especially helpful for language development.

Mediation—Sequence of Developmental Behavior

For all levels, the child improves his ability to demonstrate his mediations if he is encouraged to verbalize. Through mediation, the child learns to discriminate between things and his recollections and to apply concepts more flexibly.

Level I. At this level it is almost impossible to get a child to verbally state his associations to something which we mention to him. He may, however, point to something which he associates with something else. The child talks during his play; thus he reveals his associations to the observant adult.

Level II.   The child verbally expresses a few common associations in order to complete a simple thought (e.g., he may respond to "Water is to_____" with *swim* or *drink* or another appropriate association). By pointing, he associates common household objects (e.g., he associates a spoon with a bowl). He imagines that he plays or otherwise interacts with the objects in a picture. Similarly, he uses sand, clay, blocks, or toys for whatever purpose he intends them to be. He reveals these imaginative associations and distortions of objects when he verbalizes during play. His mediations allow him to imagine a simple action which might occur in a picture (e.g., "The doggie's running away!") and to anticipate his own possible future action as when he expresses a desire to take turns at something (e.g., "I'm going to Grandma's.").

Level III.   The child's verbal mediations increase to include abstract associations that show the uses or functions of objects. Although his longer sentences imply that he possesses longer thought units, his choice of words suggests that he mediates mainly in terms of objects and actions. He names his drawings, indicating his intent that they should be seen as objects which he has seen, although they bear little resemblance to real objects. He points to objects after hearing about their uses. Visual mediations allow the child to show associations between uncommon objects. The child talks aloud for longer periods of time, revealing many make-believe activities. His ability to control the loudness and rate of his speaking implies that he may imagine himself speeding up his own talk.

Level IV.   The child's verbal mediations extend to a description of an object by an adjective that identifies one of its essential characteristics (e.g., heavy). Training him at this level to label things increases his tendency to label. This is also true at level V. He "reads" pictures, thereby showing that he has mediations for interrelating them. He points to the correct picture after it is described to him. He visually associates objects which are related by common functions. He tends to confuse fact and fantasy because he strongly believes in the mediations which his imagination creates.

Level V.   He completes difficult verbal associations which require a knowledge of many of the essential physical characteristics of objects. His memories of past events can mediate his actions. His visual associations have become so abstract that he can imagine what is on the other side of a door. By this level, it is possible for us to appreciate the extensive part that associations play in the child's thinking.

MEDIATION OBJECTIVE FOR PRESCHOOL-AGED CHILDREN

1. To be able to form associations between pictures and verbal descriptions, between objects and labels, between objects and functions, and between past experiences and present observations.

WHAT THE TEACHER DOES

In the early preschool years, the alert teacher listens to and observes the child's verbal activity so that he can determine the associations that the child is making. Therefore, you must allow the child to talk aloud as he plays and uses the materials and equipment.

Games can be played which encourage the child to make associations. These may be oral games such as sentence completions or questions (e.g., "Boats float on_____."). Children can play matching games with small plastic items (e.g., cups and saucers, knives and forks) or with pictures (e.g., picture lotto games). You can use catalogs and magazines to provide opportunities for the children to make associations through discussing and cutting out pictures of things that go together.

Whenever possible, provide the names of objects. Children need to know the names of objects before they can give you evidence of how their mediative processes are developing. You may help them to use descriptive labels by providing activities that help children identify characteristics. The characteristics *soft* and *loud,* for example, can be developed through the use of bottles or cans. You can prepare a matching set of bottles which contains different substances (e.g., corn, sand, rocks, beans) in each set. The child shakes the bottles and matches the sounds. He can tell you which set of bottles sounds the loudest and which sounds the softest. The same process can be used with a set of cards that have a piece of sandpaper on them. The child can be given the labels *rough* and *smooth* and learn through the sense of feel what these labels mean. Although most preschoolers generally learn the gross characteristics of descriptive labels, some will be more discriminating and add adjectives such as "sort of rough" or "very soft."

Throughout the preschool years, the child will be interested in picture books. His ability to "read" from the pictures should be encouraged by "reading" with him. Name objects for him, discuss the interrelatedness of objects, and predict what might have happened before or what will happen after an event.

Since the child confuses fact with fantasy, you should realize that the child himself is confused on what is real and what is fantasy. Often, he has a misconception which he may or may not be mature enough to understand.

Problem Solving and Logical Thought—Sequence of Developmental Behavior

Level I. The child tries to fold a paper while observing another person performing the action. He retrieves an object by pulling a string. His irregular usage of plural forms signifies that he confuses the individual and the class; he cannot distinguish *all* from *some*. According to Piaget, the child has moved beyond the period of *sensory motor intelligence* and is in the period of *preconceptual thought.* Although this period is marked by the appearance of a useful level of verbal communication, the child's system of meaning is broader than language; that is, his system of meaning extends to images which he cannot express through speech. These are aspects of the representation of memory proper which frees the child to think about things previously experienced but not currently present.

Level II. He tells about a simple action in a picture. He is still confused about when to use the plural forms of nouns and verbs. He concentrates so heavily on a limited aspect of his experience that he fails to perceive many other aspects. However, this does not prevent him from doing what he can do on the basis of the limited aspect which he does perceive. If problem solving requires him to shift to some other aspect, the child very well may not be able to accomplish this. This heavy concentration on limited aspects of experience causes him to be inflexible in his thinking and problem-solving behavior. For example, if he decides that a particular person is going to show him something, he cannot accept the substitution of someone else and consequently resists learning from the substitute person.

Level III. If you ask the child to tell a story about a picture, he simply lists the objects in the picture. This does, nevertheless, represent an advancement over level II in that his naming of several objects shows that he can voluntarily shift his attention to several aspects of the picture. He is shifting his concentration or *decenter-*

ing. Decentering permits him to understand functions of objects and also what means lead to what outcomes (e.g., he gives a sensible answer to questions like "Why do we wear clothes?"). He assembles a simple two piece puzzle. The child's partial decentering of attention also makes him less rigid behaviorally. Not only can he be controlled by language but he can be entertained and begins to entertain. Usually, he begins to dream; his dreaming may result from representational thought (i.e., memory) and from a sufficient amount of decentering which permits him to focus on successive images during sleep. Insofar as dreams are confused with reality, we may judge that the child's waking thoughts may closely resemble his dreams. The child's thinking may take the form of an extensive metaphor in which he imagines himself to be a particular object.

Level IV.   The child sorts objects for likeness on the basis of perceptual similarity; responds correctly to the distinction between *some* and *all* (e.g., in response to "Are all of the bottles big?" the fact that they are all bottles will not lead him to judge that they are all also big); develops interpretations of abstractions regarding relative length, location, distance, weight, or area; answers practical questions about desirable courses of action; tells a story with a main theme, although he makes few inferences; traces a simple maze, evidencing an ability to anticipate and avoid line crossings; establishes correspondence between pairs or small sets of objects, but does not establish an ordinal series or one-to-one correspondence of larger sets.

Until now play has served the child's internal needs (assimilation), but now it begins to be an expression of reality (accommodation) as well as a distortion of it. The line between fact and fiction is thus emerging, but it is very tentative. The child's awareness of the distinction between fact and fiction is mirrored in his question, Is it real? He is at a transition between preconceptual thought and what Piaget labels *intuitive thought.* The child now recognizes that all things that look alike are not necessarily the same. The child's greater decentering can be seen in his curiosity about details, a marked improvement in drawings, and an interest in observing things from several perspectives. However, he still comprehends the distinctions between the particular and the general by first viewing a problem from one perceptual perspective and then another; this shows that he can concentrate on only one aspect at a time. He has a notion of an individual object being conserved, but he does not believe in the permanence of a collection of objects (e.g., a glass filled with beads). When he looks at a collection of objects, he may attend to the aspect of height or width but not both at once. The aspect to which he attends causes him to believe that the quantity has been increased or decreased by transferring the objects to a container that accentuates either height or width.

Level V. His associative processes have, through language, become so socialized that he gives sensible answers to questions which can be answered from an associative or mediational perspective. For example, he knows that cows or goats produce milk, although he probably does not possess a logical knowledge of the process of milk production in the cow for feeding her calf. He is not yet a logical thinker. He answers questions that require him to solve simple social or personal problems. He anticipates which pathway in a simple maze is longer or shorter and can behave in accordance with his perception. His simple maze tracing also improves, but if one uses an imaginary fence to divide the pathway into parts, the child loses the sense of the whole. The child can assemble noninterlocking puzzles; and if he knows what the object is, he persists by trial and error until he correctly assembles the puzzle. His socialized sense of congruity/incongruity lets him decide what is wrong with or missing from a picture. He laughs at some verbal absurdity. His sorting behavior is more developed than at level IV.

Inference begins to appear in the child's storytelling; he refers to elements which are not perceptible. His story may seem to be in a logical sequence. Although his answers to conservation questions (i.e., questions which require the child to examine a visible display of materials that are arranged and rearranged to provide bases for comparisons and contrasts) are not truly logical, he gives fewer wild or highly personal reasons for his conclusions. Yet, the child usually is not a conserver. What he accomplishes in this area he does by trial and error and he apparently bases his solution on a perceptual stragegy. That is, the child judges two object sets as being equivalent on their appearance to be so, or he tries to construct an ordinal series of sticks of varying length on the basis of a perceptual idea of what a series might look like. His trial and error behavior shows how much his decentering of attention permits him to view things from one perspective and then another. The fact that his process of solving problems can be disturbed by manipulation of materials shows that his solution is based on perception rather than logic. Through his play and his imitation, the child begins to understand through an active process of exploration.

PROBLEM-SOLVING OBJECTIVES FOR
PRESCHOOL-AGED CHILDREN

1. To engage in problem-solving experiences.

WHAT THE TEACHER DOES

Children's abilities in problem solving result from the experiences they have and how they are encouraged to deal with them. You cannot directly teach a child how to solve problems. The foundation for problem solving is laid with the early sensory experiences— finding out how things feel, taste, and smell—and encouraged by your questions that are designed to fit the problem-solving strategies which you think the children can use. Your questions and comments must be directed toward helping the child to solve his problem rather than giving him the answer. You must plan the situation so that the child has a solvable problem and that your assistance helps him to be successful.

Since problem solving is closely related to attention at the earlier levels, a good technique is to help the child decenter his attention from the most obvious aspects of a situation. A simple redirection such as "What about this part over here?" is helpful with children who are at level III. When the child is dissatisfied with what he is able to do, such as making something out of clay, you can ask him what part he wants to change and how he wants it to look. These statements focus on the problem to be solved and may give you a lead to the kind of suggestion that might be helpful.

Another useful technique with children who are at levels IV and V is to question, What will happen to_____if I (or you) do_____?" Concrete situations in which you can actually do what you suggest are good because the child can observe and express what happens even though he may not be able to provide a verbal answer. If your goal is to encourage problem solving, keep in mind that the actual answer is less important than the process of arriving at it. Another general technique which focuses on the process is the simple question, How could we find out?

You can propose a simple problem to solve for a child at level V. For example, with a doll house and some appropriate, small dolls you could suggest a specific situation and ask the child to show you what the dolls would do. You could balance two bottles of liquid on a scale and ask the child what would happen if you added more liquid to one of the bottles. You could sit at a table, give the children small beads or blocks, and pose problems such as: "I'm going to take these blocks. Do I have all of them? Do you still have some? Do I have more?" The child can count to find the answers to the questions. You might ask a child to draw a picture of a house. After he has completed his drawing, you could turn the picture over and ask the child to show you what it looks like on the back. Situations like these provide important insights into the child's thinking processes which can guide you in planning additional experiences. The more concrete such situations are, the more opportunity they are likely to provide for the child to learn.

chapter 6

Helping Children to Develop Socially and Emotionally

This chapter deals with those areas of behavior that are in the *affective domain*. The areas which we consider are social relations, social skills, behavioral controls, other areas of socialization, motivation, and personality. Actually, each of these areas consists of a group of related topics. Sometimes we have separated these topics in order to make the behavioral descriptions clearer or more exact. For this reason, you will sometimes find additional related topics with their own headings under the main headings that are listed above.

The *social relations* area considers how the child relates to parents, other children, and adults outside the family in terms of interest in people, feelings of attachment, competition and cooperation, preferences, dependence and independence, and typical patterns of social adjustment.

Social skills refer to those behaviors which contribute to the child's understanding of social relationships or otherwise influence his social relationships. These behaviors include imitation; understanding how people differ in age, social class, race or ethnic background, and social roles; and understanding emotional expressions which are communicated verbally and nonverbally by others.

Behavioral controls treat those behaviors which show the child's responsiveness to control by others and himself. This section also considers the child's understanding of which behaviors are desirable and undesirable, his judgments of whether something morally "bad" has happened, and the child's development of those characteristics which make him more likely to understand and follow the rules that are taught to him. The development of behavioral self-control is a major task of socialization in the young child. *Socialization* is the process by which the child comes to adopt the behaviors which are valued by his society.

Other areas of socialization consider those behaviors (besides controls) which society labels as appropriate or expected actions by the child. These include sex role behaviors; aggression, self-assertion, and dominance; maturity in self-care and in taking responsibility or helping with work; positive social behaviors such as kindness, sharing, and generosity; and humor.

We have divided *motivation* into two areas; namely, extrinsic motivation (i.e. behavior that is associated with some sort of external reward or incentive) and intrinsic motivation (i.e., responses based on internal interest or preference). When we consider extrinsic motivation, we look into the kinds of reward, who gives the reward, its timing, punishment, threats, and closely related matters. When we consider intrinsic motivation, we look at those interests which result from novelty and might be motivated by curiosity and those which result from the child's prior experience of successfully or unsuccessfully interacting with objects or being rewarded for particular behaviors.

Personality refers to the overall organization and direction of the child's behavior. It includes his individuality in areas such as temperament, creativity, and expressiveness. It also concerns the child's self-concept, his fantasy life, emotional reactions and concerns, and how he relates to the reality outside himself (i.e., his ego organization).

For convenience, references which apply to more than one level are often mentioned only for the first level to which they apply or in an introductory statement. For this reason, refer to the introduction of each section and to all five levels to avoid overlooking something which may be important to your objectives.

Social Relations—Sequence of Developmental Behavior

Overall, the preschooler at level I is emotionally attached to a small circle of adults, especially in his immediate family, and is dependent on them for many things. By the time a child reaches level V, he gives more attention and interest to other children, and he is much less in need of other people's help to accomplish what he desires or to protect him from danger. This development is evident in the child's moving away from his mother more often and making contacts with a widening network of people, including other children. This outward movement is called *detachment*. It leads to the appearance of more mature forms of attachment; it is not to be confused with emotional detachment which is a sign of serious difficulty. Participation in a preschool program speeds and smooths the process of detachment for the child.

Adult discussion with the child about those human relations topics which are used in imaginative, dramatic play improves the child's ability to relate to other children. Children who learn to give mostly positive reinforcement and little negative reinforcement to peers become more socially accepted. Parental example of reinforcement strongly influences the child's behavior in this area.

Because adjustment is mainly a social process at these levels, observation of the child in his normal social contacts is necessary. Observation of the child by himself does not provide valid evidence about his adjustment. This helps to explain why a child's behavior at home and in a preschool program may often appear to be quite different. Among normal children, about 30 percent usually have adjustment problems. Such problems are found three times as often in boys as in girls.

Level I.

General. The child forms basic attachments to parents before this time. He decidedly prefers adults to children. He is quite dependent upon his parents or other adults but is likely to want to be dependent on his own terms. He may demand attention, and he needs his mother to be present if he is to have friendly interaction with a stranger. He vigorously explores his immediate environment at home, getting out of his mother's sight, but stays near to her in a strange location. Some children prefer to stay near their mothers even when they explore at home; these children tend to be emotionally immature and are likely to be delayed in their adjustment to other children for this reason. Despite the child's continued dependency, the beginnings of detachment can be seen. Detachment arises from the child's interest in the physical environment, and he may resist attempts to redirect his behavior from exploring something dangerous. He shows anger if the redirecting attempt is abrupt.

Adjustment.   Until this time, adults have been mainly nurturers for the child. The child's exploratory movements away from the parents signal to them that he is more in need of control than of nurturing, and they begin to make demands upon him. The child responds to these changes as if he does not understand. He expects his parents to continue being nurturers, and he is not ready to adapt himself to their demands. This is the source of his temper outbursts and resistance. The child still needs to have his mother or a reasonable substitute nearby. The child's social relationships are dependent and exploitative. When level I children are placed together, they play in parallel, largely ignoring each other, and show no preference for particular other children.

Level II.

General.   Because the child at this level is capable of greater independence, his occasional strong displays of dependency may seem out of place and may often be joked about or openly rejected by some parents. He alternates between insistence upon independence and requests for adult help with something which we know he can do. Sometimes he is considered to be rebellious because he demands that others adapt to him rather than meeting them part way. He still prefers adults, although he may experience such mixed reactions to them that we say he is ambivalent; that is, he wants them and does not want them at the same time. Some adults feel so exasperated by this that they react to the child with the same insistence, stubbornness, and ambivalence, thus providing a model for the child of all these behaviors. It is a frustrating time for the child when he must learn to give up the nurturing parent that he has come to expect for a parent who nurtures and demands that the child stay within certain limits.

Adjustment.   Adults need to recognize that the child is still incapable of adapting to others' demands. His exploitative and dependent style of interpersonal adjustment continues to grow more intensely. He seems to want to view adults primarily as sources of supply, and he cannot yet understand or accept the limits which they set. If the child is with other children, parallel play continues. At this level, the child is very solitary.

Level III.

General. Often, something happens in the adult-child relationship during this level which causes things to become smoother between the adult and the child than at levels I and II. Perhaps the child now understands that his parents are still willing to help or supply but that he is expected to do what he can do for himself and to control himself.

The child does not need to have his mother present to have friendly interactions with a strange adult. Yet, children typically continue to seek physical closeness to their mothers when they are present. Dependency behaviors are decreasing in nearly all children and continue to do so through level V, although there is an ongoing tendency for children who have been more dependent in this overall period to remain more dependent later compared to peers. They also tend to be less interested in achievement but have fewer accidents, perhaps because they explore less vigorously. Some children who use less imitation may use dependency contacts to gratify their social needs from levels III through V. Dependency contacts may be expressed less directly, as when some children act naughty to get attention. Usually, however, children simply increase talking to their mothers as a way of getting attention. Dependent contacts with adults occur more often than helpful ones (see Other Areas of Socialization) through level V, although dependent contacts decrease at each level from III (dependency contacts are six times as great as helpful contacts) through V (dependency contacts are now only two times as great as helpful contacts). Children at this level who have a strong attachment to parents tend to form a stronger attachment to their teacher than children who are not as attached to their parents.

Peers are becoming more interesting and attractive to the child. Yet, the overall number of contacts with adults is still greater, even in a preschool program. Those children who often verbalize from their imagination are more attractive to other children from now through level V.

Adjustment. The adult who shows an abiding interest in the child and his activities is an effective source of reinforcement for him. Therefore, the quality of the child's relationship with his parents importantly influences his ability to adjust at this level. The child's imitating actions seem to occur more frequently when the adult is able to hold the child's attention; therefore, the quality of the child's relationship with his parents determines whether he will be able to use imitation as a means of adapting to his parents' demands.

Whereas at levels I and II the negative social attitude of the child was more prominent than his positive social attitude, this is less important at levels III and IV. Negative attitude decreases at these levels. The child continues to have an exploitative outlook, but he shows less dependency. The child seems to feel that if someone else gets his way, then he loses out. Despite this, he seems to be more adaptive to adults and hence begins to become more socialized. That is, he conforms more often to parents' demands and possibly gains pleasure from accomplishing the tasks which they set for him.

His play ceases to be strictly parallel, and we see the beginnings of social play with peers. The child prefers one particular companion, often of the opposite sex. He may call this child his friend. His improved adjustment in social relationships at this level may be due to his increased language abilities as well as to his greater understanding and imitative abilities. These changes might explain why he is able, through language, to move into social relationships with another child as well as to better accept the limits which his parents set. Interestingly, this is also the level when children first show individual and group differences in their responses to cognitive demands. For example, when children are asked a question which requires that they think and attempt to make a socially acceptable or conforming answer, socially advantaged children are more likely to do so than socially disadvantaged children. These differences in responses to cognitive demands become even greater through level V and help to explain the better early school adjustment of socially advantaged children.

The child finishes much of his early discovery of himself during levels I and II and makes some progress toward the discovery of others during level III. It is true that he knows other persons exist before this, but only now does he produce enough language to communicate with them. His experience of the conflict of his will with that of his parents during levels I and II may have prepared him to accept the necessity to give way to others at times to avoid certain unpleasant consequences; this adjustment makes it possible for him to adapt to a peer. After the child has developed socially to this extent, he has a tendency to be relatively more oriented to people (extraverted) rather than to his own interests (introverted). Individual differences in introversion/extraversion remain a somewhat stable tendency from level III onward. Beyond these basic external changes, the child still wants things his own way. His social relationships tend to be filled with a mixture of tendencies (e.g., selfishness or affection; competition or friendship seem to alternate). He can be sociable, but just for a few minutes at a time, until the next conflict of wills is brought on by some small incident. It is not surprising, in light of this, that he tries to take advantage of others when he can and may learn to manipulate others.

Level IV.

General. Certain individuals are more interesting to the child because he better meets his own needs through interacting with them; but this works for him only part of the time, so he has his ups and downs even with his favorite friend or adult. He will cooperate for a time and then quarrel. He resists children more than he does adults, perhaps because adults are able to explain why they want a particular thing. If he is in a preschool, he has more contacts with peers than with adults. Children have preferences for children of the same sex and continue to have this preference through level V. The child seems more interested in pleasing an adult of the opposite sex. The dependency of boys differs from that of girls. Girls seek to be near an adult or to get reassurance, and boys bid for attention. Overall, regardless of sex, children at this level are more likely to talk or perform to get attention and less likely to touch or hold. Children who are dependent learn more incidental things that occur (e.g., who was wearing boots), but their intentional learning (e.g., remembering the name *troll* in the story of the three billy goats) is lower than it is for less dependent children. The child often goes about the immediate neighborhood at this age.

Adjustment. The child's social adjustment is similar to that of level III. He is still exploitative but with less dependency. He believes that what others get, he loses. He is less tied to this viewpoint than before and is more able to compromise. While companionship strongly interests him, the child's will dominates his social contacts, especially with peers. Children adjust to each other by alternately cooperating and quarreling. Children who do not care for each other will not behave in this manner—they simply avoid each other. Enough cooperation occurs among friends that their social play is recognizable as cooperative. The child also seems to be wiser about child-adult relationships and will be less likely to talk to a strange adult than he was at level III. In response to his awareness that speech is intended for social communication, the child begins to talk less out loud to himself (egocentric speech). Egocentric speech drops off more at level V. Socially disadvantaged children may cease their egocentric speech somewhat later. In any event, the adult should not discourage the child's egocentric speech.

Level V.

General.   At this level, the child not only associates with particular friends but verbally expresses these preferences. Although the child tends to play with friends of the same sex more often, he is still likely to play with children of both sexes. The child is likely to ask for help when he needs it; he expresses less emotional dependence. The child continues to show a movement away from dependency (e.g., positive forms of getting attention through good performances are increasing). The child moves freely about the house, yard, and immediate neighborhood beyond his mother's direct observation, and he can be allowed to go to a familiar location outside the immediate neighborhood (e.g., to a friend's house or to school). He safely crosses streets and may explore the neighborhood. He is more competitive with his peers than he formerly was.

Adjustment.   There has been a deepening of the child's social relationships. His relationships are more reciprocal; that is, he expresses a greater amount of give and take and has a sense of loyalty to particular people. These reciprocal behaviors are limited to his family and friends. Social relationships are seen by him in terms of actions rather than in terms of feelings, motives, or relationships. His relationships with peers will generally be more adjusted than at level IV; this is evidenced by his willingness to cooperate in the use of play equipment.

At this level, adjustment is mainly a matter of conforming to social expectations. Often, girls will conform to adult standards while boys will not conform to adult standards; this shows that both groups adjust by matching their behavior to social expectations which, in this case, relate to sex typing. Some children may question adult demands for one-sided respect from a child to an adult. Others will show concerns regarding displays of affection between parents, which make them feel left out and isolated; these concerns show that they are near the end of early childhood. We are particularly concerned about the child who at this level is either withdrawn or strongly aggressive. Both of these groups of children are having difficulties in social development and adjustment.

SOCIAL RELATIONS OBJECTIVES FOR PRESCHOOL-AGED CHILDREN

1. To be relatively more oriented to other people rather than oriented to just his own desires.

2. To prefer associations with children over adults. (level V only)

3. To gradually progress from parallel to cooperative relationships with other children (with frequent quarreling).

4. To ask for help when it is needed.

5. To verbally express a preference for particular friends.

6. To move freely and safely in a familiar neighborhood.

7. To develop cooperative relationships with peers.

8. To give and take with a sense of loyalty to particular people.

9. To match behavior to social expectations which relate to sex typing.

10. To establish friendly interactions with adults other than his parents.

WHAT THE TEACHER DOES

When the child enters a preschool program, he is still very attached to adults, particularly his mother. He needs help and support from the preschool teachers and staff; this is why a high ratio of teachers per child is recommended for younger children. You must provide enough adults in the preschool to help the child in his physical needs such as dressing, toileting, and eating; to provide ideas, concepts, and vocabulary; and to give assistance in construction and art activities.

The teacher must understand how critical the adult role is in this particular stage of the child's development because the parents often do not. Because the child is becoming more self-sufficient and because parents are demanding more of the child, you should provide parents with a better understanding of their child and his conflicting need for independence and support at the same time.

You will want to provide the delicate balance that often exists between the child's dependency on you and his independence from you. Sometimes the child's needs conflict with one another. That is, he is able to do a task or to help himself, but he wants and needs your attention at the same time.

Do not encourage the dependency, but help him at the appropriate times. For example, if the child wants you to help him to button his coat, you can button one button while he buttons another.

Be cautious that you do not use the child's dependency to meet your own needs. Teachers, like mothers, sometimes attempt to meet their own needs through the behavior of the children. One of the ways they attempt to do this is through supporting a dependency by

A preschooler often needs a word of comfort and advice.

the children on themselves. You must remain objective while you demonstrate love and affection which the children need.

Since the younger child is not ready to cooperate and play with other children, you should accept his parallel play patterns and seeming avoidance of other children. Involve children in small group activities, but do not force their participation. While some groups of three- and four-year-olds can come together for music and story time, individual children who show strong resistence to this activity should not be forced into it. A suitable substitute activity can be found for them so that they do not disrupt the larger group. This behavior may be found in older children as well; it depends on their background of experiences (i.e., lack of opportunity to play with other children, dependence on mother, etc).

Consistently practice patience and firmness with the children in the classroom. Since the child imitates adult behavior, the model he sees is important. As he develops in his ability to relate to other children and adults, he will practice the behavior that is used with him. Use firmness in the sense of being consistent in what you expect of the child. For example, if the program requires all children to move to an outside area or into a larger room for large activities, be consistent in expecting the children to put away activities and move to the other area. If you allow the children to procrastinate or to dillydally, routines slip by the wayside and the child becomes uncertain as to what you really expect of him.

The program should provide encouragement for cooperative play to develop. Cooperative play cannot be forced, but it can be fostered. Asking two or three children to help you clean the art table or to put away books or housekeeping equipment serves several purposes. This activity gives you an opportunity to model desired behavior. It also brings the children together in a cooperative situation which still allows for individual endeavor. Eventually, the children will be able to initiate this behavior upon a signal or suggestion from you and to follow through on their own. This kind of helping activity should be encouraged for the children who have been playing in these areas, although others may join in the clean-up process.

The materials and learning centers in your room can serve the purpose of bringing the children together. Consider the child who is standing by the housekeeping corner but is too shy or timid to join the play activity. Suggesting a set of dress-up clothes or actually leading him to the area may provide a role for him so that he can be included in the play. Adding accessories to block areas may make it possible for more children to participate in the activity.

Another situation to be aware of is when too many children are trying to participate in an activity. Be prepared to add new activities or to help the children find alternatives within the room.

While it is recommended that children receive help with toileting and dressing, you should allow the child to do as much as possible for himself. Children should be shown how to care for themselves and encouraged to do so. If eating meals at school is a part of the program, provide utensils that are the right size for the children. Encourage them to pour juice or milk, to serve themselves from the bowls of food, and to help clean up after the meal or juice time.

Dress-up clothes that have fasteners give the children an opportunity to get in and out of clothes by themselves. Paint smocks and shirts can have large buttons or grippers so that children can help each other. If consideration is given to self-help features in the classroom, the children will be helped in their drive toward independent behavior. At the same time, children should know that they can ask for help when they need it and that they will receive help that is needed. An observant teacher knows when to give just the right amount of help and when to encourage the child to do for himself.

Children who are at the higher levels can be allowed to run small errands in the building. You can send a message to another teacher, send a child to bring a bucket from the custodian, or ask a child to show a parent to another section of the building. Of course, you must know which children can be given this responsibility, and you must be alert to the child who does not return within a reasonable length of time.

Even though you notice a decrease in the child's egocentric speech, do not expect him to work silently either alone or with others. Allow him to talk as he plays and works because his language is still developing, and this is a necessary process. If some children are especially loud in this respect, you may wish to discuss the noise level. You may also rearrange your room so that activities which seem to encourage loud, egocentric speech such as block, sand, or housekeeping play are placed apart from the quiet areas of the classroom.

Some children may pair off and spend much of their time together, but they may not really be good for each other. One may be too dependent on the other, or one may lead the other into destructive play. Find ways to separate these children at times. You may put them at separate tables for juice or send them to different groups for stories. It will not always be easy to separate children who are friends, but it often must be done; and it should be done without the children feeling that you do not want them to be together.

Some consideration should be given as to sex role expectations that you have for the children. Your expectations as well as family expectations can influence the child's behavior. Be fair in your expectations which are based on how children grow and develop and refrain from placing adult role expectations on the children. Do not force conformity on the boys although it is tempting to do so since girls at this age tend to conform more easily. Recognize each child for what he is and treat your group of children as developing individuals.

Social Skills—Sequence of Developmental Behavior

Some social skills develop within the child and then proceed outward to his understanding of others. For example, before level I, children express most of the primary emotions nonverbally. Next, they learn to recognize emotions that others express nonverbally. They may learn to name these emotions (e.g., "I'm happy"). Eventually, they understand others' statements about emotions and label the emotions which they see others express. The order of these later learnings may be somewhat different for individual children because of their learning environment, but they always begin with the child's own experience and behavioral expression of emotion. Imitation, as a social skill, begins within the child before level I; Piaget referred to it as *sensory-motor* imitation. During the preschool years, the child's social progress through imitation will depend greatly on two things: (1) the quality of his social-emotional relationship with his parents, and (2) the particular behaviors that these models demonstrate. The child learns about particular social roles and about how people differ in age, social class, and race or ethnic background differently than he learns imitation and emotional recognition skills. At first, the child shows no tendencies in these directions, and his cognitive development prior to Level I makes skill development in these areas almost impossible. He uses cognitive skills to learn in these areas like he does in other types of concept learning.

Because the development of social skills follows these basically different patterns, we expect to find many children who show a mixed rather than a matched group of social skills for their level. This cautionary note will help to avoid some possible confusion. When the child's social skills seem to be mixed in view of his overall developmental level, we can usually understand why in terms of what other influences affect each particular group of skills. You will find these guides to be helpful:

1. Delays in imitation or in the nonverbal understanding of emotions may suggest that something is interfering with the child's attachment to or basic emotional relationships with others.

2. Mislabeling or delay in labeling of emotions (when nonverbal understanding is present) usually indicates how the child's family uses language to talk about emotions.

3. Delays in social skills which are learned as concepts will most likely relate to the rate of the child's overall cognitive development.

These three rules do not explain all of the mixed variations that you might see, but they should help you to understand many of them.

Other facts that will help you to understand how social skills develop are as follows. Children from different regions of the United States have different developments of racial awareness. If the child at levels III through V has faulty beliefs about race, he can easily form more accurate concepts. The child's entrance into a program with children who differ from him in social status increases his awareness of these differences. The child at levels III through V frequently imitates his parents' aggression, dominance, and use of power, even under conditions that are not favorable for imitation. Imitation operates most efficiently as an incidental learning process and may be disturbed if the child is requested to copy intentionally, although to have his close attention is essential to imitation. Paying attention to the child or rewarding him tends to capture his attention and thus his imitation. The child imitates those things which he has seen rewarded or attended to by adults with another child (this is called vicarious learning), and he imitates the positive behaviors only under those conditions that are highly favorable to imitation.

Level I.   The child nonverbally recognizes others' emotions and seems to be aware of whether they are favorable or unfavorable with regard to his own desires or intentions. He cannot reliably label these emotions. He imitates simple motor behaviors (e.g., a crayon stroke) which he may not do spontaneously or upon request without a demonstration. Imitative motor behavior is prominent in his language; he imitates both himself and others. The child remembers through imitation. He often follows his mother and tries briefly to do whatever she is doing. The child is not aware of social status concepts at levels I and II. He knows the words for close family relationships, strongly asserts his ownership and rights, and understands what belongs to whom. Thus, at this level, ideas about property ownership and "my" territory substitute for a knowledge of roles.

Level II.   The child begins to recognize which person's face is *happy* or *mad* when the adult uses these labels in his questions. Imitation increases—the child now stacks blocks following a demonstration and perhaps with some encouragement. Imitation of self and others continues to be used in the repeated practice of things which the child is mastering. The child makes reference to others' things as *his* and *hers,* but he does not appear to comprehend the concept of maleness or femaleness.

Level III.   The child consistently recognizes the labels *happy* and *mad,* and recognizes (but less accurately) *afraid, sad,* and *disgusted.* The child depends less on immediate demonstration and may imitate something which happened earlier. In fact, he sometimes imitates better after he has observed someone model a behavior than he does at the actual time of observing it. From now through level

V, the child's imitating behavior is influenced by how rewarding the model is. Children who have observed racial differences comment on them, thus revealing their awareness. Often, children from low income families are not aware of social class, but children from middle income families may be aware of social class. In free play, however, children give little evidence of preferences which are based on race, social class, or other signs of social status. Most children are beginning to be aware of what is judged by adults to be sex typed. This development begins a little sooner among boys. A few children can imagine what something would look like if they were seated and viewing it from a different person's perspective. Being able to do this is a sign that the child is moving away from his personal (egocentric) perspective toward adopting the perspective (i.e., role) of another person.

Level IV.   The child recognizes the facial expressions of fear. Some children recognize the facial expression of surprise. Sadness is now recognized from the tone of voice alone without familiar words. After children have learned these labels, they understand what someone else means when he, for example, says, "I am happy."

The child imitates more difficult actions like that of a person who is folding paper; the child can match a simple pattern of two folds. He can imitate or pantomime from memory. The child will imitate a peer who has been rewarded. At this level, children boast about their parents and may quote them to support something which they believe. A rewarding, attentive parent will begin to see the child's imitation of his own positive social behaviors. Children's racial awareness increases, and they recognize age differences on the basis of size differences. The child associates sex role labels (i.e., man, woman) with stereotypes about hair length, clothing, etc. In his response to simple questions, the child shows that he knows children do not and cannot change their sex, although more complicated questions about sex changes confuse him. He regularly uses, with come confusions, pronouns which refer to sex.

A few more children can adopt another person's spatial perspective of something, but many children cannot do this at this level. The child is partly learning how roles may differ in terms of places; for example, he knows that people live in homes and go away to other places to work. The child recognizes how someone else feels much sooner than he recognizes how things would look from someone else's perspective. Because of this, when we want to reason with the child, we must rely on an appeal to his understanding of how others feel. This may help him to adapt to another child's anger, fear, or jealousy.

Level V.   From viewing faces, the child can recognize disgust. He recognizes, with some accuracy, who is interested or ashamed, but he does not recognize contempt. If a child does not know the label for a particular emotion which he sees, he can tell whether the person who is shown has a pleasant or an unpleasant expression. If an adult uses a particular label for an emotion, the child often begins to use that label in his conversation. The emotions of cartoon characters can also be recognized, although the emotions displayed by human faces were understood earlier. This is the first level at which some children who at first misunderstand a cartoon character's facial expression will make a more accurate second guess after they have had a chance to see the cartoon placed into a cartoon story, thus we see that a story context now begins to add to the child's accuracy of emotion recognition. Some children will know from facial expression, verbal label, tone of voice, and context how someone feels. Sadness is recognized from tone of voice alone and anger begins to be recognized from voice. The child does not recognize happy or affectionate feelings from tone of voice alone.

If the child is shown an already constructed, patterned chain of beads, he cannot copy them as well as he can if he has seen a model make the pattern. At this level, the child may remember an event better when he has had a chance to imitate or pantomime it. He picks up entirely new motor behaviors quickly in this way. His imitation is linked to his curiosity; he uses imitative play as a way to learn about the challenging realities of the social world. For this reason, the child primarily imitates adults (i.e., because they are the powerful representatives of the mysteries of social reality) and imitates peers only a little.

The child recognizes age differences on the basis of facial cues and is no longer deceived by size differences that do not match someone's age. He recognizes that there are differences between the rich and the poor and that ethnic groups differ in appearance or speech. Racial attitudes may be present. He knows the common family roles and imitates them in play. He is learning about many roles outside the family, particularly those that relate to the world of work. He has improved in his ability to judge what something might look like from another person's spatial perspective. He knows that what another person might feel in a particular situation would not necessarily match what he would feel. He has, therefore, lost some of his egocentricity in the area of emotions. His belief that men and women do not change sex is firmer now. Toys and other objects which are typed as feminine are more easily recognized as such than those that are typed as masculine. The child does not view most activities as being sex typed (e.g., helping around the house is not seen as sex typed).

SOCIAL SKILLS OBJECTIVES FOR PRESCHOOL-AGED CHILDREN

1. To imitate the behavior of significant adults and peers.
2. To be able to label emotions for which labels have been supplied.
3. To use imitation in order to learn about the realities of the social world (e.g., to practice "going to work" or "making the supper").
4. To recognize the emotions of characters in cartoons and picture stories.
5. To recognize how someone feels from observing his facial expression, verbal label, tone of voice, and context.
6. To have a general grasp of how another person might feel in a particular situation.
7. To be aware of family and occupational roles.
8. To be aware of social differences such as age, sex, race, speech and appearance in ethnic groups, and socio-economic levels.

WHAT THE TEACHER DOES

As a teacher, you must be fully aware of how significant adult behavior is in relationship to the child. His social skills can be enhanced or deterred depending upon the behavior of the adults who interact with him. This becomes especially important in the preschool setting when the teacher knows that the social skills that are being developed in the home are not adequate for the child's interaction in the world outside the home.

With this in mind, demonstrate those behaviors which help children become sensitive to other people's feelings; teach children how to share, to have patience, and to cooperate in group endeavors. While these characteristics are developing and cannot be expected to be demonstrated overnight by the child, you must keep the goal in mind as you work with the children. It is easy to become discouraged when guiding this facet of development.

Since children learn about adult roles through imitating the actions of adults, you should provide many opportunities for the imitation of adult roles in your classroom. The importance of dramatic play was emphasized in the language section of this text and should be reemphasized here for a different reason. A classroom that provides props such as hats for various occupations and dress-up clothes (e.g., apron, men's work shirts, men's and women's shoes, etc.) will encourage the children to act out the behaviors of the adults that they associate with the clothes. If the children frequently ride buses to town, they can imitate the bus driver. They may imitate clerks at the supermarket or a service repairman who has been to their house. You should acquaint yourself with the community of the children so that you can provide dress-up clothes that will give the children the opportunity to imitate what they know best.

You will also want to enlarge their experiences through books, films, and field trips. These activities should include a discussion of the people they meet or see and how these people are helpful to others. It may also be appropriate to discuss when people are not helpful to others.

If you label emotions, preschoolers will begin to recognize these emotions and use the labels. Say to the children, "Does he look surprised?" "My, you have such a happy face today," or "Sally looks unhappy because she just fell down." There are many opportunities in a preschool classroom where you can help children to identify emotions. Pictures of people displaying various emotions are available from many sources. You can also find many good pictures in popular magazines. Make these pictures available so the children can look at them on their own as well as with you.

You should also discuss the children's feelings in real situations, such as when a child has fallen down, has been surprised, or has been frightened. Talk about feeling sad or feeling happy. As you discuss these feelings, call attention to your facial expression or the expression on the child's face. This response should be spontaneous, such as when a child surprises himself at the washbowl after he squirts or splashes water in his face. Looking in the mirror, you can say, "Look at the surprised look on your face. You surprised yourself." When two children have a disagreement and are angry, you might talk about the angry look on Tommy's face. Pictures and cartoons sometimes allow for these discussions more readily than actual experiences.

You can guide the child by discussing how he would respond to someone who feels sad, happy, afraid, or angry. Sharing a new toy, asking someone to play, or even leaving someone alone can help the child as he learns to interact with others.

You can provide positive experiences for the children which will foster an awareness of age, sex, and racial differences. Many parents and grandparents are more than willing to come into the classroom and interact with the children. Some will have special talents or special interests that they can share such as crafts, hobbies, and cooking experiences. Others will be willing to read to the children, tell stories, or play games. Do not set up these experiences to teach about age, sex, race, or ethnic groups, but set them up for the purpose of the children having a positive experience with someone who is older or of a different race or ethnic group.

Behavioral Controls—Sequence of Developmental Behavior

Preschoolers have a better understanding of what is "bad" behavior than they do of what is "good" behavior. Children who are emotionally reactive may develop controls somewhat later than those children who are nonreactive; however, highly reactive children may feel just as much or more shame or personal disappointment when they do not behave as well as they or their parents expect. From level III onward, children who break a rule display face and body tension. The child who is at levels III through V is likely to develop behavior controls under the same conditions which were described as being favorable to imitative learning. Behavioral control development also requires that adults communicate explicitly what they expect from the child and that they then consistently enforce this. Children misbehave when things are not made clear to them. Mild threats are more effective behavior controls with socially advantaged children than strong threats which are likely to increase their negative behavior. The opposite approach is more effective with socially disadvantaged children. Apparently, the adult who overemphasizes by strong threat is modelling out-of-control behavior for the socially advantaged children. Socially disadvantaged children, on the other hand, believe that the adult does not mean business unless there is a lot of emphasis. The development of behavioral controls is generally a part of overall maturity, although socially disadvantaged children may develop controls more slowly because of their early environments. Behavioral controls develop under those conditions which relate to identification (i.e., the process of wanting to become like one's parents and accepting the standards which they set).

Level I.

Behavior. The child does not yet know which behavior is good or bad. He responds mainly to physical stimuli and may be difficult for the adult to control. He may stop what he is doing in response to "No" (sometimes "No! No!" will be more effective), but some children respond by doing more vigorously what they were already doing when ordered to stop. The child may resist if he is told to stop, but he will start a new behavior on command. Therefore, it is easier to redirect him to something new rather than to get him to stop everything.

Character. He does not yet understand that his parents have wishes to which he must conform. Instead, he sees people as sources of action. For this reason, he is able to respond to threats of action (i.e., to threats of retaliation). He has no understanding of rules, and his responses to outside controls are lacking or undependable. His time orientation is the present, so he cannot wait or remember a warning for very long. His newly discovered motor abilities allow him to get into everything and to experience himself as having an almost omnipotent will (i.e., he seems to believe that he can do whatever he decides to try). His impulses to action conflict with others, and he is too young to understand explanations.

Level II.

Behavior. He responds to *bad* but does not respond to *good*. He is a bit easier to distract and may imitate something else which is modeled for him to do. He stops to a single command of "No" or "Stop," and if he does not stop, he will not vigorously increase what he is doing. It is easy to get his cooperation by modelling or telling him to do something else.

Character. He thwarts his own desires mainly out of a desire to please his parents and to avoid punishment. He appears to be more interested in his activities than in people, which means that his parents must be clever to get him to behave. Parents who use only force and no cleverness may teach the child rebelliousness or may cause him to be overly submissive. Most parents are now insistent about at least some of his behaviors, and they communicate to the child that they expect him to respond to their demands; this challenges the child's sense of omnipotence, but he continues to act on his own impulses. Not surprisingly, many parents feel that if they ignore his behavior, they will harm the child's character. Actually, too much insistence by parents has negative effects at this level.

Level III.

Behavior. The child may understand *good.* If he is asked whether he did a particular thing, he is very likely to respond *yes,* especially if it is a socially acceptable action. He does not reliably say *no* when the action about which he is being questioned is undesirable, although he says *yes* less often to such questions. His behavior contrasts with his apparent understanding of bad, but it does not contrast with his understanding of *good.*

If the child repeats aloud to himself an order to stop, he is much more likely to stop what he is doing. However, he cannot use a rule about when to stop. He can stop what his parents tell him to stop. Both boys and girls conform to their parents' orders now and at level IV. They have become fairly easy to control verbally. The child follows simple directions to perform more than one action; this shows how memory contributes to his behavior control.

Character. The child's omnipotence now disappears; he seems to recognize his parents' wills and power and makes an attempt to adapt himself to them. The child views others not only as sources of action but also as sources of wishes or demands. This is an important step in his overall social development. You may recall that this is the level at which the child begins to ask *who,* and his interest in people increases greatly. The child's desire to conform may seem high. If you refer back to levels III through V of the "Social Skills" section, you will see how the development of imitation runs parallel to that of character. In some senses, this is the beginning of what is called *identification.* It is an identification which relies on conformity to avoid punishment or to maintain favorable relationships. This level of conscience depends on the parents' wishes being communicated and enforced. The child complies with only those demands which are forced upon him. He gets away with whatever is allowed. For this reason, his conscience is sometimes called *expedient* or *opportunistic,* and his orientation has been called *premoral* because it is based on his paying attention to obeying to avoid punishment. You will also see similarities between this and the child's social relations at this level. The child's increased amount of time perspective of past and future causes him to remember how his parents reacted *before* and therefore to understand how they may react *now*. If they have been inconsistent in their behavior, he is uncertain of what will happen.

Level IV.

Behavior. The child's tendency to respond *yes* to questions about desirable behavior is a little higher than at level III, but his tendency to respond *no* to undesirable behavior is the same. He responds appropriately to simple questions about what a person should do in certain situations. He knows simple abstractions about people (e.g., pretty, brave). He can on the basis of this respond to internal or psychological forms of praise or verbal control which is used by adults (e.g., "That's a *brave* child."); this makes adult control easier than when only *good* or *bad* can be used. He voluntarily pays attention on request and acts on command. He is likely to carry through requests or commands because he does not become distracted easily. He follows three commands about the same as he did at level III, although his ability to use greater psychological abstraction may improve his self-control if he happens to label his behavior (e.g., "I'm doing fine," or "I'm nice"). He still needs adults to be very explicit about what is forbidden. Often the child will more easily conform to rules in a game if he is playing with an adult of the opposite sex.

Character.   Peer relationships are becoming more important to the child, which may explain why his desire to conform to adult standards does not always appear quite as high. Children's moral judgments about problem situations show that they do not understand people's intentions. For example, they believe that an accident which causes a lot of damage is worse than an intentional act which causes only a small amount of damage. Many children will say that a child in a story is bad just because he has been punished. They favor severe punishments for others (e.g., criminals); they do not have the idea of reforming someone. They do not reason that you should treat others well because you want them to treat you well. The child knows the rules but obeys them for the immediate benefits of obedience (i.e., for praise, rewards, avoidance of punishment). He is still expedient or opportunistic. There is no true evil for him; something is bad only if one gets caught. Children tell tall tales and may believe that these are lies only if adults overhear them. Boasting may be the child's way of showing how strongly he identifies with what he has learned is good or worthy of praise. This is not so much lying as it is pride in a child with active imagination. His growing perspective of future time may help him to tolerate frustrations (i.e., he knows they will not last forever) and to wait.

Level V.

Behavior.   The child now understands what common behaviors are desirable about 80 percent as well as he will understand them when he is an adult. He still understands what is bad better than he understands what is good. He now tends to respond *no* to questions of whether he behaves undesirably. He still does not often use terms such as *sweet* or *hard* to refer to the psychological characteristics of people, but he does this more often than he did before this level. These terms may further increase the effectiveness of language as a reward or punishment.

The child follows his own directions for behaving in certain ways. Later, this self-direction will become internal, but now we still hear the child speak out loud when he is using language to control his behavior. For a few children, the language of self-control has already become internal and silent. The child can sit and keep from moving about much better than ever before, but he still needs to move about freely when he reaches his limit. He is less bothered by distractions than at level IV. He accepts rules in his play, although he may, at times, concentrate so heavily on his own wishes that he fails to recognize that a rule applies. He generally conforms to adult wishes; he does somewhat better if his actions are observed fairly often. He may express a feeling of loss, shame, or disappointment when he breaks a rule. Children tell fewer tall tales, but some children deny obvious mistakes. Many children still break a rule or cheat if something seems excessively important or attractive to them; this includes picking up things which do not belong to them. If the child is angry or otherwise overly emotional at the moment, he is more likely to yield to temptation. Usually, girls hesitate twice as long as boys do in temptation situations, showing a greater conscience development. Girls conform more to parents and boys conform more to peers.

Character.   Based on differences in conformity, girls' conscience appears ahead of boys' conscience. This difference, however, may mean that both girls and boys are behaving more in sex roles, with girls conforming more to parents and boys conforming more to boys. Some children spontaneously quote rules and otherwise show how much rules guide their behavior. Those children who behave this way and who conform have reached a beginning of what is called a conformist level of conscience. Many children are still mainly expedient. Other children behave sometimes by conforming and other times by conforming only if they are being observed or think they are being observed. The child who is at a conformist level of character development obeys rules for more external reasons (i.e., from fear of disapproval or punishment) than internal reasons (i.e., internal means to obey rules simply because one has come to believe they are inherently right, binding, or authoritative). This fact agrees with a parallel observation about the child's commands to himself; he must still command himself (i.e., give self-directions) aloud because his internal or silent language is too weak or subject to distraction to regulate his actions. They are obeyed because they are the rules more than from fear of punishment. The minority of children who are conformists conform to receive rewards and to have favors returned. They are, thus, more concerned with maintaining good relationships with their parents and other adults than with avoiding punishment. Expedient children also see others as sources of favors, but they are more concerned with threat. The conformist level of conscience is based on what Lawrence Kohlberg has called *naive instrumental hedonism.* This term means that the child has a simple (naive) idea of how good behavior leads to or is instrumental in producing pleasure or satisfaction (hedonism).

The child reflects longer before making choices or acting. His concept of time develops further; he can wait longer for a reward. A few children begin to recognize motives or intentions in others; this shows that they are aware of these tendencies in themselves and are more advanced in character development. Generally, the child does not yet realize that a person's moral judgments about degrees of goodness and badness are relative to his personal values. He unquestioningly accepts the rules which are laid down by adults as truth. This partly results from the child's belief that adults act only from kindness or benevolence; only a few children have begun to question this. Children often believe that a child must have been bad or he would not have been punished (compare this with the view at level IV). Children see some misfortunes as punishments by God.

BEHAVIORAL CONTROLS OBJECTIVES FOR
PRESCHOOL-AGED CHILDREN

1. To respond to redirection better than to punishment or direct attempts to stop undesirable behavior.
2. To increase his ability to respond to verbal controls.
3. To become increasingly able to use self-direction in controlling behavior.
4. To use language as a means of controlling his behavior.
5. To increase his ability to understand what is meant by "good" behavior. (See levels I through V.)
6. To respond positively to insistence on "good" behavior. (The child may react negatively to over-insistence on "good" behavior.)
7. To conform to demands when it is known they will be followed up.
8. To obey and conform in order to avoid punishment.
9. To obey and conform in order to maintain favorable relationships with adults.
10. To have a simple idea of how "good" behavior leads to personal satisfaction.

WHAT THE TEACHER DOES

As a teacher of young children, you must be clear about what behavior is expected of the children. First, you must be clear in your own thinking and, second, you must convey this to the children. Making this distinction is important because it is not always necessary to make a verbal declaration of what behavior is expected. You can accomplish a great deal by stage setting; for example, you can plan a situation in which the children are invited to behave in a desirable manner. A teacher does this when he sets up activities on a table before the children enter the room for a session. He also uses stage setting when he introduces new activities to attract the attention of children who are beginning to be disruptive. This technique of redirecting the disruptive child's behavior is the basic technique which is used when opportunities for choice are available to the children.

The establishment of a routine also helps to clarify to the children what behavior is expected of them. Beyond that, children gain a sense of satisfaction from knowing what is expected of them and being able to do it. This involves such simple things as carrying out activities in the same order each day so that the child knows that music, story time, or rest follows the cleanup after the activity time.

You must stop behavior that is unsafe, clearly out of bounds, or disturbing. Your ability to stop such behavior is an absolute requirement to success in teaching preschool children. In other words, you must be able to set limits because the children have not reached a level of development that is necessary to limit their own behavior. Since the preschool child is responsive to adult disapproval and punishment, you must use them sometimes; but because children have so many socialization skills to learn, you are advised to use preventive techniques. Teaching techniques which are most effective are planning new and interesting activities every day, planning so success is assured, redirecting behavior that is about to become disruptive, planning shelf space so putting away is easy, providing more than one popular toy such as a tricycle, providing choices of activities, and starting a new activity when children have tired of those which are available.

If you feel that children should not be allowed to throw sand, watch the number of children in the sandbox because too many children leads to disputes and disputes lead to sand throwing. See to it that each child has a shovel and some other equipment. If there seems to be a problem, move near the sandbox. Older preschoolers will sometimes discuss their problem, and you can help them work it out. With younger children, you can note the source of difficulty. If a child throws sand, you can state the limit and the reason for it (e.g., "I can't let you throw sand. It gets in children's eyes, and it hurts."). If the children are able to respond to a verbal reminder, they may stop the sand throwing. If the child continues to throw sand, you may need to reinforce the verbal reminder by removing him from the sandbox with the explanation that he can play somewhere else but that he can return to the sandbox later when he can remember not to throw sand. Your action expresses your disapproval, identifies something the child can do, and clarifies the conditions under which he can return to the sandbox. Furthermore, it makes him responsible for making the decision. Many children will almost immediately say, "I won't throw sand," and go back and play peacefully. How long the child stays out of the sandbox is not the point at issue; the issue concerns throwing sand so if the sand throwing stops, the goal has been accomplished. In a sense, the removal from the scene is punishment and children recognize it as such. Do not make the mistake of saying that the child may not play in the sand for the rest of the week. Immediate and short-term punishments are more effective with preschool children. If you set a long-term punishment, you will also be punished in the long run because you have to enforce it to make it effective.

A problem that many teachers face with setting limits is that they speak too soon and then change their minds when the child starts to protest with kicking and crying. Think before you act, but once you have set a limit, enforce it. If your expectations are realistic and your enforcement is consistent, the children will soon learn that there are situations in which conformity is necessary. This is a fact of life, and you must help preschoolers learn it through their gradual maturing and your consistent treatment. Sometimes it helps you to set reasonable limits if you try to view a situation as the child views it. Ask yourself questions such as, What is the child trying to do by his behavior? What purpose does the behavior serve for the child? or How does the situation look to the child? Sometimes, if you ask these questions, you will act differently than you would have if you just looked at the situation from the adult's point of view. If you understand the child's motivation, you may be able to suggest an alternative activity that will be acceptable to him in accomplishing his purpose.

The reason punishment is seldom used is that it only stops undesirable behavior or causes the child to feel inadequate. Punishment does not help him handle the situation better the next time.

The child learns behavioral control by careful guidance. You must teach him some techniques to use with other children when he wants to get something that the other child has or when he wants the other children to do something for him. You might say, "Ask Jimmy for the truck when he has finished playing with it," or "Did you tell Sue that you needed someone to help with the building?" Such comments give the child a suggestion.

Since the child's conformity is highly dependent on maintaining favorable relationships with the teacher, the teacher's presence is often important in controlling behavior. For example, a child may be able to maintain control if you move close to him when he is about to misbehave. Under these conditions, verbal control may not even be necessary. Sometimes a look of confidence or gently touching the child will help him to maintain control.

The eventual goal of using self-direction in the control of behavior carries implications for the program. Children can manage a great deal more freedom when the program choices are appropriate and when the demands of the situation are consistent with the child's purposes. When the expectation is too high or too low, the situation creates frustration. The program should increase the child's motivation to want to behave acceptably and his feeling of satisfaction with being able to do so.

Although the child is in the process of learning what is "good" behavior and what is "bad" behavior, this occurs almost automatically in the process of learning rules at home and school; and you do not emphasize it in the classroom. Your responsibility is to develop a classroom atmosphere where all children feel accepted. This is easier to accomplish when children behave in ways that are considered "good" rather than those that are considered "bad". Your greatest problem in this area is with children who engage in a lot of out-of-bounds behavior. By getting the child interested in classroom activities and by planning as many positive contacts as possible between you and the child, you should be able to reduce conflict situations in which you must intervene to help him control his behavior. This is the way that you can help the child to feel accepted even though you cannot accept all of his behavior. Since many children have already begun to think of themselves as "bad," the process of change is very slow; but if you can avoid the acquisition of the label "bad" in the classroom, this is a positive move. With all the corrections of behavior and approval and disapproval that children inevitably receive, there is little chance that they will not learn what is "bad" behavior and what is "good" behavior as soon as they are cognitively able to understand the concepts.

So far, the emphasis in this section has been on working with individuals within the classroom. There are also skills to be learned about working with the class as a whole. In order to provide adequate guidance, you must have an awareness of the total classroom. If you learn to consciously look around the room and note what each child is doing, it will soon become a habit; and you will be almost unaware that you are doing it. Part of the reason you need to do this is to judge the timing of the guidance that you give the children. A suggestion that is given at the right moment is usually accepted by the child, but a suggestion or comment that is made too soon or too late is often rejected by him. Often, your proximity to a child reinforces his acceptable behavior while your apparent lack of attention encourages him to engage in out-of-bounds behavior. Behavior that is becoming too noisy or in which children are beginning to argue and quarrel with one another soon goes from bad to worse if the teacher does not attend to it at once. It is constantly necessary for the teacher to make decisions regarding when to intervene and when to let children handle their problems. If you handle all of the problems, the children will not learn to do it themselves. On the other hand, there are times when some children are successful in handling their relationships with other children in quite unacceptable ways. You have to make a careful appraisal of the kind of learning that is involved before you decide which role to take. Some teachers are quite successful with individual children who have difficulty with classroom management. Both your classroom guidance and work with the individual are very important to helping children develop behavioral control.

Other Areas of Socialization—Sequence of Developmental Behavior

AGGRESSION/ASSERTIVENESS

Parental permissiveness, excessive punishment, and modeling of aggression lead to aggressive behavior in children. Whenever a quiet child, who is at levels III through V is attacked, attacks back, and is reinforced by being successful, he is likely to aggress again. Therefore, his total amount of aggression may increase.

Levels I and II. The child aggresses only when he is frustrated— usually by an adult. Usually, a tantrum results. The child's aggression is undirected or self-directed (i.e., he bites or otherwise hurts himself). As the child approaches level II, he may aggress against an adult when he is frustrated. He begins to make threats. Aggression is almost nonsocial at these levels.

Level III. The child's threats increase. Tantrums may continue but are generally less frequent. If the child is with other children, he may aggress against them. At this level, this is usually the child's way of making a social contact because his language is still limited and physical means of contact are easier for him to use. Adult models (especially male models) increase children's aggressions, and a male peer model may increase boys' aggressions. The aggression that is displayed in cartoons causes the children to be more aggressive.

Level IV. The child still uses aggression to establish social contacts. Some aggression on the child's part is a sign of his assertiveness or tendency to dominate. This is a peak level for the expression of aggression. Children now commonly criticize and try to boss one another. Assertiveness over others is a frequent play theme; this may come out in the child's insistence that the other child play a less desired part. By now, assertive and submissive behaviors become stable; therefore, the same children are likely to behave the one way or the other. Assertiveness at levels IV and V appears to be related to later intellectual assertiveness. The same conditions of modeling operate now that operated at level III.

Level V.   At this level, there is an overall drop in aggression in most children's groups. Of course, children who have had little or no prior peer contact will at first increase their aggression. Children who have been in a group situation before and still aggress persistently are immature and less able than their peers to enter into social relationships. Aggression is more likely to be expressed under appropriate conditions (e.g., when children compete over scarce materials). Boys show more aggression against people and objects; girls' aggressions are more verbal and may involve tattling. Girls' nonimitative aggression is high and boys' imitative aggression is extremely high. Both boys and girls are expressing more controlled, verbal, and indirect forms of aggression than they did earlier.

SEX TYPING

Parent-child relationships (see influences favorable to imitation under Social Skills) and parent availability and expectations are the main influences on this area of development. Girls who have all sisters tend to be more feminine and boys who have all brothers tend to be more masculine. (See Social Skills regarding children's recognition of and beliefs about sex differences.)

Levels I and II.   Sex-typed behaviors are essentially absent, or they are at a minimum.

Level III.   Sex-typed toy preferences may begin to appear, although boys and girls often prefer the same things. An adult's presence or absence has no bearing on this.

Level IV.   Children make more sex-typed choices of objects.

Level V.   The child adopts a sex role, which conforms to the standards that adults expect. Sex-typed toys are preferred by boys and girls. A boy is less likely to choose an inappropriate toy for his sex if an adult is present than if he is alone or with other children. Sex-role adoption is also shown in children's tendency to play mainly with peers of the same sex. The child tends to imitate adults of his sex. No preferences for sex-typed activities are present, except those that arise from particular toy choices. Children increasingly use boy and girl dolls in play to represent their classmates.

MATURITY/RESPONSIBILITY

The fine motor requirements for these behaviors are discussed in Chapter Four. Mature behavior increases among children who are in preschool.

Level I. The child asks for and needs help to use the toilet. The child unzips. He is usually dry during the day but often wet at night. He may also wet during naps. He uses a spoon and fork, drinks from a cup, requests food, and gets a drink. He undresses himself and tries on adult shoes. He washes his hands when he is told to do so. He helps to pick up or carry things when requested to do so and does these things in imitation.

Level II. He still needs help at the toilet. He begins to dress himself but needs help. He unbuttons those buttons that he can reach. He dries his hands after washing them but needs help. He helps to put things away; imitation is effective.

Level III. The child usually stays dry at night and cares for himself at the toilet. He can pour a liquid and is neat at the table. He buttons those buttons that he can see; slips shoes on, but often on the wrong feet; and dresses under his parents' supervision, although he does so more independently. He washes his hands without help, but he still does not thoroughly dry them. He begins brushing his teeth. If reminded, he uses extra caution to prevent breaking things, and he helps adults with small chores. His helpfulness toward adults increases through level V, but dependent contacts with adults outnumber helpful ones at all of these levels.

Level IV. He goes to the toilet by himself and is dry through the night, except for accidents. Occasional daytime accidents may occur when the child is ill or too busy playing. He is a skilled eater; he may try to butter his bread and begins to cut food with a knife or fork or both. He dresses himself without supervision; he buttons, laces shoes, but cannot tie a bow. After a reminder, he washes and dries his face and works at brushing his teeth. In order to keep his gums healthy, he may need help to brush his teeth at least once a day. He likes to help with adult activities if the adult is nearby and will carry out a small errand.

Level V. The child cuts foods that are difficult to cut. He may tie his shoes and surely wants to learn. He dresses and undresses without help, although he still needs help to find his things. He brushes his teeth fairly well on his own, needing only occasional inspections; takes a bath, but needs help to get really clean; and brushes or combs his hair. He does longer errands, will put things away in storage if it is easy to use, and is considerably more cooperative. He is becoming more competitive at the same time. He may go to bed alone when told to do so and can be trusted with a small amount of money to keep or spend for what he desires. However, parents should not always expect to be happy with what he buys.

POSITIVE SOCIAL BEHAVIORS

Level I. The child does not share. His play is solitary or parallel. He will sit and listen to a story. He enjoys playing very simple motor games (e.g., clapping each other's hands). His interest in his siblings is not usually great, but he responds well when they approach him, unless they tease him.

Level II. He often looks at other children when they play, but he generally does not approach them and does not share. His interest in siblings remains low, and he may quarrel with them.

Level III. With adults, he spontaneously shares experiences, chatters about what is happening, or asks questions. He may perform for an adult. His contacts with peers increase if there is an opportunity, but his contacts with adults stay constant (see Aggression/Assertiveness). He spontaneously begins cooperative play, at times getting himself involved in true interactions, and can share certain toys. It is easier for him to share what he does not want. He understands taking turns, but it is not easy for him to do so. He may tease his older siblings, especially if teasing is modeled to him.

Level IV. The child shares information and impressions, asks many questions, and talks to himself and others. He enters into competitive fine motor and gross motor games. He cooperates with his peers, but within the limits already suggested in the discussion of aggression/assertiveness. Children at this level are quite sensitive to cues for cooperation and competition, and their sharing can be increased by social reinforcement. The child's spontaneous helping behaviors toward peers are rare. Children imitate their parents in their social play with other children. A nurturing father who helps around the house seems to be the most powerful model for helpful behaviors.

Level V. The child expresses appreciation or gratitude. He plays simple games and can often resolve quarrels without outside help. He decidedly prefers peer companionship over adult companionship and will play well with children. He shows kindness toward those whom he likes, expresses sympathy and concern, comforts the upset child, and may try to protect a young child or pet. These advances must arise from the child's increased ability to decenter (see Attention and Problem Solving in Chapter Six). These developments often make their first appearance in the child's dramatic play. In his play, he rehearses many positive social behaviors (e.g., settling quarrels, helping others), which he cannot yet use in the full heat of real-life competition. This type of play activity not only provides rehearsal of particular behaviors but also helps him to adopt the perspective of others, as he takes turns playing different roles.

HUMOR

Levels I and II. The child laughs in response to his own actions or to those of adults. He may laugh in imitation now and through level V. His laughter may occur in connection with teasing or around the performance of forbidden behaviors.

Level III. The child laughs during social contacts with peers. His laughter over socially unacceptable behaviors now exceeds that over motions by himself and others.

Level IV. The child may laugh over slapstick, silliness, and a lack of congruity in the appearance of something or someone (e.g., a cartoon character with a giant body and tiny legs and arms). His humor is thus beginning to be in response to cognitive sources.

Level V.   The cognitive trend of level IV advances further. The child may respond with laughter to silly or absurd statements. Humor based on wit, puns, and double meanings is still beyond the child's comprehension.

SOCIALIZATION OBJECTIVES FOR PRESCHOOL-AGED CHILDREN

Aggression/Assertiveness

1. To exhibit controlled forms of aggression.
2. To exhibit aggression verbally rather than physically.
3. To use more indirect forms rather than direct forms of aggression.

Sex Typing

1. To be better able to identify feminine sex-typed objects and masculine sex-typed objects.
2. To conform more to the standards that are expected by adults in regard to sex typing.
3. To increasingly imitate adults of the same sex.
4. To show a preference for sex-typed toys.

Maturity/Responsibility

1. To become increasingly able to care for himself at the toilet with fewer day and nighttime accidents.
2. To become increasingly helpful to adults, especially when actions can be imitated.
3. To dress and undress himself with increasing responsibility.
4. To become increasingly willing to feed himself and handle eating utensils.
5. To increasingly handle responsibility for himself (e.g., washing hands, brushing teeth, having money).

Positive Social Behaviors

1. To become increasingly able to interact with peers, to share information, to cooperate with activities, and to converse.
2. To grow in his ability to share and take turns.
3. To be increasingly able to settle quarrels and differences by himself.
4. To engage in more competitive situations.

Humor

1. To laugh at his own actions and those of adults.
2. To laugh at silly or absurd statements.

WHAT THE TEACHER DOES

Aggression/Assertiveness. You should expect, and in some cases welcome, a certain amount of aggressiveness and assertiveness in the children with whom you work. Your role is to determine when the aggressive behavior of a child will harm others. Since aggressive behavior is often the child's means of social approach to other children, some of it is necessary. Too often aggression is stopped before children have a chance to work problems out for themselves. Older preschool children can handle their differences easier than younger preschool children, but some of the older children may still be in the early levels of development.

When it seems that the children cannot solve their differences, discuss the problem with them. If it is one of sharing a toy or game, suggest ways that both children can use the object. Sometimes it helps to have basic rules such as, "the child who has the toy first may use it first," or "whenever you leave the toy, someone else may come and play with it." Taking turns can be very difficult for some children and often is the source of aggressive behavior.

Some children may dominate others in play situations. You may join in the play situation and suggest role changes, particularly in housekeeping and block play. You may find that the submissive child is content with the role that he has been given which is another reason for suggesting change; he, too, needs to change his position in the group and needs your help to do it.

You may be able to suggest changes without joining in the play situations. You may be able to discuss the behavior with the child and bring about changes. Since the children who are at levels IV and V show verbal aggression instead of physical aggression with other children, you will need to help them control their verbal outbursts. At the same time, you must recognize that verbal aggression is developmental and more desirable than physical aggression.

When one child consistently dominates another, you may want to introduce other children into the play situation. When you know the personalities of your class, you can bring children together whose behavior can complement one another: thus, the behavior of another child can help to manage the aggressive behavior of the child that you are concerned about.

There may be times when the aggressive child should be removed from the group. Many factors should enter into such a decision, and other developmental characteristics (see Behavioral Controls, Temperament, and Personality) should be considered before this step is taken. A general rule to follow is to remove the child when he is threatening harm to other children and when you cannot possibly talk with him in the classroom. When this happens, there should be enough adults in the classroom so that you can go with the child, calm him down, and talk with him about what has happened while the other adults supervise the group.

Sex Typing.   Provide a wide range of toys and materials that will allow children to make sex-typed choices. Children of both sexes should have the opportunity to choose toys or materials which are for either sex. Children should not be forced into any sex-typed preferences at any of the levels (i.e., boys should not be forced to play with dolls but neither should girls). Encourage children to try a variety of toys and materials. Include children in different activities involving sex-typed materials such as the doll area or the moving vehicles and blocks.

Some children live with only one of their parents. If possible, provide staff members of both sexes for these children so that they have an opportunity to be around adults of both sexes. If staffing is not possible, then volunteers or resource people, particularly males, can be a regular part of your program so that fatherless boys and girls have some contact with both sexes.

Toys and materials should not be labeled as being only for girls or only for boys. The children should feel free to play with any material.

Maturity/Responsibility. Consider each child individually as you try to develop maturity and responsibility. Determine as early as possible which self-help activities each child can manage. Discuss with each mother just how much responsibility she gives to her child. Some mothers will encourage three-year-olds to dress themselves and allow or make them do as much as possible for themselves. Other mothers continue to dress their children until they are five or six years of age. Parental expectations play a significant role in how children care for themselves.

Children are quick to let you know if they need help with toileting. However, be alert to the quiet child who may be too timid to ask for help. At no time should a child be scolded for asking for assistance. The reasons for needing assistance vary and should be respected. Be positive and encourage self-help. Sometimes a child only needs to be shown how to care for himself and praised for being successful to become self-sufficient at the toilet.

Usually, the child learns how to dress and undress, use eating utensils, brush teeth, etc., in his home. However, many homes do not or cannot provide the experiences needed for these activities. Provide for such experiences whenever possible, giving as much assistance as is needed and encouragement and praise as well.

You can foster responsibility by encouraging children to put away toys after they have finished playing with them and to help you clean up after art, juice time, etc. You must recognize that some children will resist clean-up time; but if you are kind and persistent, you can encourage their cooperation. It is difficult for children at levels I, II, and III to complete a clean-up operation. You will obtain more cooperation from the children if you work along with them and if you make a game of the activity. Be realistic in your expectations for specific children.

Positive Social Behaviors. These behaviors seem to be a composite of many others which were already discussed in this chapter. If the child is to develop positive social behaviors, you must provide ample opportunities for his interaction with peers. Scheduling should be flexible with many opportunities for children to establish small work and play groups where they can plan together and play together. You should set up experiences which require the children to wait for turns or share materials. The level of the children's development determines whether these groups should consist of two to three or six to eight children.

It is significant for you to recognize that these skills are in a stage of development and that many children are in the very early stage. You will be guiding much of this development through the entire year, and you may not see the fruition of your efforts until very late in the year or the next year. This is not an area in which you can expect instant results.

Humor.   Humor should be a part of all early childhood classrooms. If the child is to develop a good sense of humor, he must be exposed to humorous situations and see good humor exhibited by his teacher. You can provide humorous experiences through your choices of stories, films, records, and fun times with the children. Laugh freely with the children, and discuss the humorous aspects of the pictures or experiences that you are sharing with them. Help them see the humor in situations that could otherwise be sad or unhappy (e.g., avert attention from a skinned knee by asking what happened to the floor or sidewalk). This kind of diversion technique must be used carefully, depending upon how serious the situation is.

You can use labeling to help the child understand the reasons for humorous incidents. Talk about why an incident is funny, silly, absurd, etc. This should be a spontaneous activity, which suggests that the teacher should be alert for many kinds of humorous situations.

Motivation—Sequence of Developmental Behavior

EXTRINSIC REINFORCEMENT

At all levels, it is easier to prevent unwanted behavior than it is to stop it once it has started. If you catch the child before he acts, he will better remember his mistakes if he is told about them immediately. Calm adults usually help children to remain calm. How well punishment works for young children depends on the quality of the adult-child relationship and the child's emotional reactivity. Punishment teaches the child only what you do not want him to do. You must use other techniques to teach him what to do. For this purpose, use modeling and imitation techniques. You probably should not use extrinsic reward when the child imitates well enough to learn new behaviors by imitation. You should use extrinsic reward when the child is not motivated, when modeling will not work, and when the behavior change is important to the child's progress. Extrinsic reinforcement is better for intentional learning; intrinsic reinforcement is better for incidental learning.

Reward is most effective when the child knows exactly what is expected of him and can see the relationship between his behavior and the reward, the reward is in plain sight, the reward is attractive to him, he has the maturity and skills to perform or stop the behavior in question, and the reward immediately follows the performance consistently. Modeling often helps to show the child how to get started even when a reward is necessary. At levels III through V, the process of rewarding is more effective if, after the child performs consistently as desired, you begin to delay the reward slightly and to talk about waiting. When the young child is beginning to comprehend, reward him. Do not wait until he has done something perfectly. Repeat this process as often as it is necessary. When he is making any progress, a reward will encourage him to keep trying until he succeeds. Do not model incorrect behavior to the child because he may copy it. Do not draw his mistakes to his attention unless you want him to stop what he is doing. Revealing information about failure to the child tends to have the same effects that punishment has upon the child during levels III through V (and maybe at levels I and II); therefore, sparingly reveal such information unless the response is totally wrong. At all levels, use words of approval generously when it is appropriate to do so. In addition to its many other positive effects, giving approval under these conditions (i.e., when you are giving extrinsic rewards or when you are modeling and the child is imitating) eventually causes the child to be more responsive to social approval and less in need of concrete reinforcement (e.g., raisins and toys). For some disturbed children, approval may produce negative reactions; in such cases, you should avoid giving approval.

You need to decide which extrinsic reinforcers are effective for the individual child. What works for one child will not necessarily work for another. Find out what appeals to the child by observing his preferences for incentives (e.g., candy, raisins, tokens, toys, and activities); you can do this by asking questions like, Would you like to do this or this? or Would you like to have this or this? After you have asked a child to make several of these comparisons, you can be fairly sure of what things or activities will motivate him. Extrinsic reinforcers tend to lose their appeal after a while so you need to reevaluate this from time to time. Never try to guess what will be reinforcing; investigate. Keep records of progress whenever you use reinforcement. Know what you are doing when you use extrinsic reinforcers. If you inconsistently use or misuse reinforcement techniques, you can actually cause serious damage to the classroom climate and to learning.

Level I.   The child responds to adult approval and to the threat of punishment, but you must have his attention. His memory is underdeveloped, so immediate reward is essential. At levels I and II, redirection is more effective than punishment for stopping unwanted behavior.

Level II.   The child still responds mainly to adult approval and threat of punishment. Adult attention causes the child to continue what he is doing. You must capture the child's attention and provide immediate feedback.

Level III.   Everything that holds true for level II holds true for this level. The child responds to expressions of love and affection and to statements that he is acting like or is like his parents. If the adult-child relationship is good, withholding adult attention slows down the child's undesirable behavior; but if the relationship is poor, withholding attention does not produce this result. His memory is developing so he can learn to delay. From now through level V, disapproval has the same effects as punishment upon the child.

Level IV.   The child increases behavior when he receives approval, and he decreases or stops behavior when he receives disapproval. Concrete reinforcers like bubble gum and candy are more effective than verbal praise. Token reinforcers (e.g., earning points or chips) can be used.

Level V.   If the child knows how something is supposed to look, he works toward producing it by trial and error. Therefore, not only modeling but also the use of a toy model, a plan, or a design may effectively guide him. When the child receives positive reinforcement, he continues to increase the behavior which comes just before it. Reinforcers have different effects on different children because children vary widely in their preferences. At this level, children are generally moving toward greater responsiveness to social reinforcement (i.e., praise or disapproval). They also respond to abstract forms of social reinforcement (e.g., "pretty," "brave"—see Behavioral Controls, levels IV and V). Revealing information to the child about failure is still not helpful, except to slow down or stop behavior. Token reinforcement is effective and should be considered for use with impulsive children or those who are highly distractible. The effect of the threat of punishment depends on the child's prior learning history. Those who have experienced mild threat (i.e., some socially advantaged children) control their behavior after a mild threat; those who have experienced harsh threat (i.e., some socially disadvantaged children) resist temptation better after harsh threats. We must appreciate and respect the child's history and those things and conditions to which his personal history has made him responsive.

INTRINSIC MOTIVATION

All of the rewards which were mentioned in the previous section are intrinsically interesting to the child. If they were not, they would not work as reinforcers. In the previous section, we considered how to use these rewards to get the child to do something he could or would not do otherwise. When we talk about intrinsic motivation, we are referring to what the child does just because he wants to do it. Things can be intrinsically interesting if they are challenging and if the child's prior learning history has caused them to be preferred. For example, children learn to prefer sex-typed objects because of their learning histories rather than from the challenge of a curiosity, or a child prefers green squash over yellow squash because his family has taught him to like green squash. The child displays individual preferences for foods, colors, toys, story themes, and role positions to be played. Children who lack many preferences or interests have special developmental problems and later have difficulty making choices. There is a third source of intrinsic motivation. Because of the child's overall developmental level, doing certain kinds of developmental tasks may motivate him. This resembles the idea of challenge; but in this case, the child is more than just curious. The child seems to experience his life's major tasks as challenges for him to master. For example, even before he reaches level I, the child is intrinsically motivated to master the use of his body. Some of this motor development continues into early childhood, but at a slower, less frantic pace. Play, of course, fills most of the child's waking hours and is the medium through which many of his needs are expressed.

Level I. The child's independence and curiosity needs are dominant; he tries to find out what he can explore and do, and he reacts against his parents' attempts to limit his exploration. His attention is held by whatever attracts him; that is, he has no voluntary control over his attention. He wants to touch things, bang and shake them, and perhaps take them apart. The repetitive and sensory aspects of play appeal to him. This repetition suggests that novelty does not appeal to him as much as understanding what things are and how they work. He asks the names of things. He explores his immediate environment and will stay in one place if he has things that attract and hold his attention. He experiences and expresses desire, more often nonverbally than verbally. He can be willful, saying "no, no" and running away; the child's willful behavior is evidence of an intrinsic motivation.

Level II. The child's independence and curiosity needs still dominate. His exploration of the immediate environment increases, but repetition, sensory experiences, and familiarity are still his preferences. He can pay attention to something when an adult requests him to do so. He expresses the desire to do what someone else is doing.

Level III. He is less insistent on exploring forbidden parts of the environment and has become more interested in people. However, his need to explore continues even though he avoids some forbidden things. His needs for love and affection are more evident. He desires to do what his parents do and imitates their actions. He is strongly interested in getting attention from adults. Some children experience conflict between their motives for dependence and independence. He is using his visual and tactile senses in unison to explore. He is motivated to produce those actions which can be seen or imagined. He shows his willfulness by making demands and giving commands. Peers are contacted at this level, but without urgency.

Level IV. The child needs peer companionship. The child may display and assert himself over others. The child's need for adult affection display is probably as great as before, but it seems less obvious. The child becomes interested in things outside his immediate experience. He wants to make things. He has more control over his attention, so he has some ability to become interested in something if it is presented and explained to him. He selectively pays attention to certain aspects of objects (e.g., their color or shape).

Level V.   At this level, many children seem to want to maintain smooth relationships with adults, and their need for adult approval is obvious. Their interest in people is high. The need for constant adult attention, however, decreases. The needs to compete, to strive, and to achieve are appearing in the more mature children. Dominance needs increase in boys. Children learn about things through touching, looking, or asking questions—these are three different styles of curiosity which can be seen at level V. New and challenging things capture the child's attention.

MOTIVATION OBJECTIVES FOR PRESCHOOL-AGED CHILDREN

Extrinsic

1.   To be responsive to adult approval and punishment.
2.   To be responsive to concrete reinforcers.
3.   To be responsive to social reinforcement.
4.   To imitate behavior which is modeled by the adult.

Intrinsic

1.   To be interested in exploring the immediate environment.
2.   To be interested in being like his parents.
3.   To want to make things.
4.   To become interested in something that is presented and explained to him.
5.   To want to maintain smooth relationships with adults.
6.   To show curiosity by touching, looking at things, or asking questions.

WHAT THE TEACHER DOES

Extrinsic Reinforcement.   It is wiser for you to use modeling and imitation for teaching new behaviors when the children are responsive to these techniques rather than to use concrete reinforcement. Remember that preschool children learn much behavior through observing the behavior that is modeled by adults; however, preschool children do not distinguish between behavior which should be imitated and behavior which should not be imitated. Therefore, be careful of the type of behavior that you model.

While it is true that concrete reinforcers may be used effectively at level IV, it is also true that responsiveness to social approval represents a higher level of performance; and children who have been trained to respond to rewards have to be retrained to respond to praise or disapproval. You should use concrete reinforcement only when children fail to respond to other methods and when they are disruptive or disorganized. Extrinsic reinforcement is not a panacea, and you should not use it unless you know what you are doing because it can be damaging as well as helpful.

One of the most important attributes that you should have is an awareness of your own behavior so that you know when you are rewarding a child's behavior. Teachers sometimes defeat their purposes by rewarding the wrong behavior. For example, if a child who wants attention makes a disturbance at nap time and you spend the rest of the nap time soothing him, you can expect him to continue this behavior. If you call too much attention during story time to misbehavior such as hitting, pushing, or standing in front of someone, the misbehavior is likely to become worse instead of better. If a child teases you about coming in off the playground and you chase or seem upset by it, he may make a game of this behavior. While it may seem unsafe, you usually come out better if you simply state, "The rest of us are going inside," and head toward the door. Usually the child will watch to see if you mean it and then he will say, "Wait for me."

The use of approval is very tricky because of the great need for attention that some children have. Do not encourage children to seek your approval for everything that they do. Often, with some children, it is sufficient if you stand near the child who is painting, without offering very much, if any, comment. For the same reason, the use of disapproval is equally tricky. It is often necessary for the teacher to deliberately ignore misbehavior which the child is obviously using to gain attention. As long as other children are not being affected by the misbehavior, you may gain more by ignoring and finding a way to redirect it.

Intrinsic Motivation.   The approach to preschool education that we have been describing relies heavily on intrinsic motivation for success. If the program is successful, you will be able to get the children to want to do some of the things that you think are right for them. The activities that you plan should invite the children to explore the materials and objects that are in the environment or encourage them to try new activities or engage in familiar activities until they have perfected them.

Children's interests vary widely, but usually in any group, there are children who are attracted to interesting things that you can bring to the classroom. These children can help to spark the interest of the other children who are reluctant to explore. You will need to assure some children that it is all right to pick up the bunny or to shake the box with a mysterious object inside. For some children, it may take a long time for them to do more than pat the bunny while you hold it.

Some children can never seem to find things that interest them without suggestions. You will need to make suggestions for them but with the assurance that they will gradually find an activity for themselves.

Your initiation of activities is important in several ways. It gives the child a model to imitate; and since the child usually likes the activities, it helps him to view adults in a helpful role. If the child sees the teacher as being helpful to him, he is likely to have a positive response towards him. Children's interests are only as broad and as deep as their experiences. There are many things with which they have had no experience that may interest them. You can open up a whole new world to children of limited experiences.

After the children have established a basic curiosity and have become able to discuss their observations, you can begin to involve them in small group experiences such as cooking which require some explanation on your part and some shared activity by the children. Often, they become interested if there is a product to be eaten or with which they can play.

You should look at the children's interest in making things from their point of view. Although the child will sometimes make things that the teacher directs him to make, his chances of frustration and disappointment with his ability are very great when he fails. You should let him decide how the things he makes should look, even if they are not recognizable. Whether the child makes a block building, a clay bowl, or builds a simple airplane, he will have some idea of how he wants it to look. Often, he will need your help to accomplish his purpose.

Personality—Sequence of Developmental Behavior

TEMPERAMENT

This section is not divided into levels because the child's individuality in temperament appears before level I and continues during early childhood. Children differ in the following temperamental areas. Some are more active while others are less active. Some react more strongly while others respond less strongly to stimulation. Children tend to approach or withdraw from new things. They may react to weak stimulation or only to stronger stimulation. Some have negative moods while others have positive moods. They may have a capacity for strong or weak interest in things (attention). They may be distracted or they may be distracted only with difficulty (ability to be redirected). Some are able to adjust to new things while others have difficulty making new adjustments. They are either predictable or unpredictable in important body functions (i.e., bowel, bladder, hunger, thirst, sleep requirements). Children come with all combinations of these possibilities; the particular combination is a major source of the child's personality. Because these traits are a permanent part of the child, they should be respected. Nearly every child can make progress during early childhood, within the limits of his own temperament, toward dealing effectively with a wider number of realities in his environment. His temperament does not change, but his behaviors change.

Adults can help the child regulate his temperament by deciding how much and how many kinds of stimulation the child experiences and the rate and frequency with which new things are introduced into his environment. If you can and are willing to regulate the classroom environment in these ways, you will help to prevent some severe behavior problems which result when the child's temperamental needs are ignored. When children become overstimulated, help them to release tension, to relax, and to regain emotional control. You can use the child's other behavioral capabilities to accomplish relaxation and emotional control (e.g., his language, attention, motives, and gross motor skills).

CREATIVITY/EXPRESSIVENESS

From level III onward, children begin to express creativity through play. If you provide rich opportunity for the children's play, creativity will increase. Perhaps a mastery of sensory experience at levels I and II leads to later creativity in the child, but this cannot be determined from available studies. We know of no particular amount of creativity which is desirable; therefore, if the child exhibits an increased tendency to create, we must view this as progress.

Levels I and II.   Little is known about the child's creative abilities at these levels. The repetition in the child's play makes it difficult to decide what is new or creative about it.

Level III.   The child paints or draws more recognizably and constructs things from play materials; therefore, his creative expression is developing. He is no longer mainly concerned with movement and exercise; he is also concerned with producing something.

Level IV.   The child's constructive play is more prominent and is supported by his fine motor progress. The child engages in social play, thereby revealing to us what is going on in his imagination. He may boast, showing pride in what he produces.

Level V.   The child's constructive play is less frequent, and his work that relies on fine motor skills seems to depend less upon his imagination and more on his attempts to copy. In his social play, he still relies heavily on imagination. At this level, children who have been identified as being creative increase their expressiveness when they are in a room which has a rich and varied environment.

SELF-CONCEPT

From level III onward and sometimes even earlier, children make references to what they can do. The child's positive statements tell us about his self-concept. His spontaneous comments are more valuable than those which he gives in response to an adult's question about the same subject. At all levels, the child's self-concept is more positive if he has the experience of mastering important developmental tasks.

Level I.   The child who is at level I tests the limits of what he can do. He recognizes his image in the mirror; identifies himself by name; says *me, mine,* and eventually *I;* points to smaller parts of his own body when he is requested to do so; names the obvious body parts of himself or a doll; and walks with assurance. He does not know his limits or realize that he may be injured. Some of his resistance to the limits which adults set probably results from his not being able to adjust calmly to all of the things that he is able to do.

Naming himself and saying *I* suggest that he sees himself as an object and has a genuine self-consciousness.

Level II.   The child talks about himself; recognizes a photograph of himself (more difficult to recognize than a mirror image because it does not move when he does); uses maleness or femaleness when referring to himself; names and points to parts of his body; knows the labels for the less commonly named body parts; gives his full name; usually uses pronouns accurately when referring to himself; uses the two sides of his body independently; and runs with assurance. During levels I and II, he learns that he can affect his environment.

Level III.   The child's most commonly used word is *I*. He reliably refers to himself with the correct pronouns; can correctly answer the question, Are you a girl or a boy?; describes his actions while performing them; whispers or raises his voice; speeds up or slows down his speech; and darts about and throws overhand. If he is asked to draw a person, he draws a head and may add one feature, perhaps the eyes. His change in attitude toward social relationships causes him to be concerned with acting like adults. The child's desire to be more like adults implies that he accepts or adopts their frame of reference, including their verbal evaluations; he is thus in a position to have their evaluation of him become a part of his self-concept.

Level IV.   The child improves his drawing of the human figure. He can tell the front from the back of his clothes; knows the functions of his major body parts; boasts; and uses rhythm in actions, although he cannot make both sides of his body work together in rhythm (e.g., his skipping is ragged).

Level V.   The child's drawing of the human figure shows the body and the head as separate parts. He completes an incomplete human figure in several essential respects; knows his age and may know his date of birth; coordinates the two sides of his body in rhythm; can stop movement at his own command; assembles a simple puzzle of a human or doll figure; and learns the difference between left and right, if he is taught. He imagines himself in a role and plays that role. He may say what he wants to be when he grows up. This idea is still a very simple one, in which the role is empty (i.e., he does not know what psychological traits such as *kindness, helpfulness,* or *orderliness* that he wants to possess).

FANTASY

While playing, children reveal their concerns, uncertainties, fears, and questions. Themes of death and loss of parents which appear in playing activities are too common among young children to be ignored. Through playing out these themes increasingly at levels III through V, the child takes on a more realistic viewpoint. The child, when playing with dolls, expresses what concepts and other cognitive processes he cannot yet explain. In stories, children mainly depict themes of violence, followed in number by themes concerning friendliness, food and eating, and people being harmed. At levels III through V, they show an increasing sense of location or space (e.g., from home to neighborhood). They increase their use of more and different kinds of characters. They mention mothers more often than fathers in stories.

Level I.   The child's visual memory is developed enough to support imagination. He talks aloud to himself and carries out simple make-believe activities; however, his play is functional (i.e., it has more to do with repetition and practice than with imagination). At levels I and II, his mental life is very simple and restricted.

Level II.   The child interacts in storytelling, filling in or identifying what he recalls when questioned. He talks during his play about what is happening or what has just happened. He imagines that he plays or otherwise interacts with objects in pictures (e.g., "I eat you!"). He uses objects for what he wants them to be. He places doll furniture into appropriate groupings in rooms and may play with dolls. Most of his play is still functional and may seem to be more of a ritual than before. He is only beginning to express associations; therefore, his fantasies are limited.

Level III.   The child engages in constructive play, and he may engage in some dramatic (imaginative) play, although this is uncommon. His functional play decreases. He talks to himself about what is happening; this talk reveals many make-believe activities. If the child is given a picture and asked to tell a story, he instead names what is in the picture. He may imagine himself to be some object (e.g., chair) and carry on this play for a considerable length of time. Imaginary people and things show up in his play. His real home and family are his most popular play topics for levels III through V. His associative thinking has increased and his memory advances. He begins to dream and confuses the dream with reality. Children who engage in a lot of doll play fantasy are less aggressive and dependent in real life.

Level IV.   The child tells a sensible story in the correct order. He has a visual memory for the order in which things happen and can imagine a story from a series of pictures. He tells a story with a main theme. Children, especially the mentally gifted ones, have imaginary companions. He expresses ideas that are based on personal experience, confusing fact and fantasy. He begins to realize that fact and fantasy are different. He pretends to be an adult. More children take part in dramatic play. Constructive play is still prominent and functional play has almost disappeared at this level.

Level V.   After hearing a story just one time, the child recalls its main details. He tells original, fanciful stories. When he describes a picture, he is less bound to the details and is more likely to make up a story. He acts out stories in detail. Constructive play is disappearing and dramatic play is prominent. Adult life is the main theme of dramatic play. Children's dramatic play is more likely to be social now than it was at level IV, with two or three children taking on different roles. If the child's play is interrupted, he later tries to pick up where he left off. Santa Claus still seems real to the child, and

Teachers can guide children in their dramatic play.

• his understanding of death is quite simple and sometimes quite wrong. At levels IV and V, children's overall interest in fantasy (or their avoidance of it) stays fairly constant. Those who are involved in fantasy play are the more mature ones.

EMOTIONAL REACTIONS AND CONCERNS

During the preschool age, the child's unrealistic fears decrease and he becomes aware of real dangers. Of course, different children will fear different things because of their individual learning histories. If the child has an unusual emotional reaction repeatedly under the same kinds of conditions, asking about his history will sometimes uncover the meaning of his behavior.

Level I. By this level, the child is able to express nonverbally the primary emotions and some of the complicated emotions (i.e., fear, anger, sadness, joy, jealousy, disgust, affection, shame, and interest). Anger and temper are his most common emotional states. If the child cries a lot, he is expressing anger or pain rather than sadness. He also uses negativism to express anger. Tantrums are frequent. The child may be attached to a particular toy or object; is afraid of dark or strange places, noises, animals, sudden movements, pain of being struck, objects, and harm to his body—in decreasing order; gets very tired, upset, or happy (not just a little); may become jealous of other children when his parents give them attention; is not quite as distractible as before; and has better control over his emotions.

Level II. The child is wary of dark places and unfamiliar things— they cause him to be very alert or attentive. He refers to his internal states (i.e., cold, sleepy, tired, hungry, thirsty, hurt) only when they are present; is upset by other's mistakes; may stutter when excited; may be rebellious; is difficult to distract or redirect; thinks details are very important, so he is upset by shifts or changes of routine; clings to something familiar when he feels insecure; strongly shows what he feels; and often shows internal conflict over approaching or avoiding the same thing. The same things produce fear in about the same order at this level as they did at level I.

Level III. The child is afraid, in decreasing order, of active animals, unusual appearing people, noise, strange things, body harm, pain, sudden movement, and specific objects. This order shows a change from levels I and II. His voice may quaver. He has started to dream and he may express his fears through dreams, with frightening dreams increasing at levels IV and V. The overall number of fears peaks and levels off. His angry crying and tantrums of levels I and II also reach a peak and start to decrease. If he has tantrums, the child is more likely to injure himself than he was at level II. He is likely to attack; this is a replacement for the tantrum. He is likely to be aggressive over the issue of possession of a toy or object. He may express jealousy and affection toward a younger sibling. He develops interpersonal feelings toward others. His mood in peer contacts becomes increasingly positive, but his mood with his teacher becomes increasingly negative. The child releases his tensions mainly through motor activity and uses language very little for this purpose. Some of the child's insecurities at this level seem to be related to the child's concerns about withdrawal of adult affection or about their possible displeasure.

Level IV.   The child's fears are decreasing (except when related to dreams) and are associated, in decreasing order, with animals, noise, body harm, strange things, pain, and sudden movement. The realistic fears are thus becoming more prominent and the unrealistic fears are decreasing or have almost disappeared. The child is much more verbal about his feelings; this way of reacting replaces his former outbursts. He is more likely to explain his behavior than to lose control, or he may talk animatedly with lots of facial expressions about his frustration. As his outbursts decrease and his emotional verbalizations increase, he begins to have an internal reaction to emotions which affects his body functions. These are called *autonomic reactions.* The most prominent autonomic reactions are in the stomach and bowel, so an emotional upset at levels IV and V may cause an upset stomach or an accident of bowel or bladder control. His anger may be expressed as impertinence, which often seems more threatening to adults than his earlier motor outbursts. Adults often react to the child's verbal challenges as if they threaten their control of a children's group, and they judge the child to be "cheeky" or "off limits." Children accept his aggressive advances but adults do not recognize this fact so they try to stop his aggression. Approximately one-third of all emotional outbursts are associated with anger, but these are short-lived. After he expresses intense rage, the child may soon be in good spirits and acting silly. His verbal expressiveness permits him to express pride or to boast about things that he previously could only express nonverbally. His boasting may give the impression that he is self-centered. However, he seems to be less wrapped up in himself and begins to show concern for others. This is probably a result of his decentering.

Level V. The child's fears are likely to come from realistic concerns about injury or pain, although he may still have other types of fears. Fearsome dreams, however, are at a peak, and the child may not be able to get back to sleep. A majority of adults have emphasized emotional control and children are now more capable of it, in terms of their ability to talk about feelings. The increase of body feelings in the stomach and bowel gives the child internal signals about how he feels and makes it easier for him to experience feelings mentally. At this level, his verbal expressions of emotion remain very simple and often contain references to how things should be (i.e., they moralize as much as they allow themselves to experience feelings); the result is that the child has much greater emotional control. The child may appear to be more poised. These developments make it possible for the child to conform to the culture's sex-role expectations. Boys control their public expressions of fear and needs for affection; girls show less anger. Unfortunately, the child often gains emotional control at a considerable cost to his current and future emotional and even physical well-being. One sign of this is that many children at this level frequently have muscle spasms (tics). These results appear to be especially great for very emotionally reactive children and for those children whose ability to verbalize their feelings develops slowly or who are prevented by their family's characteristics from expressing feelings, even at home. Children at this level often show feelings of concern for other children or animals. Children also experience shame or guilt when they are caught breaking a rule or when they fail.

EGO DEVELOPMENT

The child's ego development is the result of his cognitive and motor development and his individual temperament as these have interacted during his personal learning history with the important social and emotional experiences of: 1) being cared for and protected by others, 2) becoming able to do things for himself, 3) moving about and exploring independently, 4) learning to control first his body, next his behavior, and then his emotional reactions, 5) accepting adult expectations and interference, 6) relating to adults and peers, and 7) learning some things about the physical and social worlds and the world of ideas. There are several similarities between ego development and behavioral controls. This is because behavioral controls and cognitive skills are aspects of ego development.

Level I.   The child has many impulses, and he has difficulty controlling them. These impulses come from his body feelings (sensory experiences) and his curiosity. It apparently takes the child quite awhile to experience and learn all that he wants to know about an object. For this reason, he repeats, persists, and practices. He also dislikes and resists adults' attempts to introduce new things to him or to redirect him. His interests are overly directed or concentrated in certain directions, but this is, of course, his method for learning about and mastering the things to which he pays attention. He can be described as being impulse ridden.

Level II.   The child is very much like he was at level I. We can learn a little more about his perceptions by observing and listening to him. When we do this, we learn that he centers his attention on certain things and misses the rest. The result is that he perceives inaccurately. He knows a little more about his experiences of internal drives, so he can tell when he is tired, hungry, or cold. Throughout levels I and II, the child is learning what he will be allowed to do and when he can expect his parents to interfere with his explorations. This is part of his learning about independence. The concept of possession or ownership is an important part of this development. If the child knows what is his, he feels more secure from interference. That is important because he perceives so many of the actions of others as inferring with him.

Level III.   The child is a little more accepting of change. It is interesting to note that he accepts change better at the same level that his concepts become more mature. Before level III, it is difficult to see even the beginnings of the child's development of the important concepts; now we see them. His visual perception for real objects is more accurate. If he looks at ink blots or other jumbled forms, he recognizes better what they resemble or are like. Before this level, there is little relationship between the shape of an ink blot and what he says it is. He confuses living things and inanimate objects no matter whether he looks at real objects, pictures, or ink blots. For example, he may pretend that he is a table, or he may decide that the rug likes him because it feels pleasant to him. He also says and believes that some nonliving things cause other things to happen. He begins to think associatively, which may explain some of his incorrect ideas about things being causes. He adapts more easily to adults, and he begins to recognize their wills as being separate from his. Thus, he becomes concerned with not getting caught, with control, or with getting an advantage.

Level IV. The child accepts change much better. His world has become more social, and he shifts his energies from learning about the physical environment to learning about social relationships. He is still concerned with not getting caught. He seems to do this a little more skillfully than before; maybe he recognizes how different his viewpoint is from an adult's viewpoint (e.g., he believes a tall tale is a lie only if it is told before an adult). Therefore, he is more cautious about who is around when he does certain things. There are several behavior areas in which we see the effect of his increasing ability to decenter. At this level, his visual memory for sequence is present, and he begins to form concepts proper. When he describes an ink blot, he refers more often to details; he may seem to be too sure of himself, which relates to the boasting quality which we discussed earlier. He has moved from forming very global impressions of things to looking more at the parts which together make up the whole. His perspective is so new to him and contrasts so much with his earlier ways of viewing things that he is overly sold on it. This may be the source of his seemingly excessive sense of certainty.

Level V. Through levels III and IV, the child has apparently been adapting to the direct influence of adults. Now he understands this influence as less personal—his parents and teachers are the source of rules. He seems to view his task as having to conform to the rules rather than having simply to conform to adults. These rules are as yet only partly internal (i.e., inside the child's conscience), so he still needs to have others around to enforce the rules. He begins to relate to others in a reciprocal manner (i.e., he treats them nicely because he wants them to treat him nicely). This is like the idea of making a trade or an exchange. He cares what others think of him, so he avoids what may offend or anger them. His social relationships may thus be called conformist. He is much less impulsive than before, and he seems to be able to slow down and think briefly before answering a question or making a statement; this development depends on his having available memories, perceptions, and associations upon which to reflect. The child's memory is almost fully developed; his perception is accurate and permits him to solve problems which can be handled through perception. He can accurately describe inkblots and frequently includes personal (i.e., self) references in his descriptions. He cannot yet apply rules to solving problems but depends instead upon moving by trial and error until he matches his perception. He does not completely decenter his attention, but he can redirect it enough to view a problem in turn from one viewpoint and then another. This recentering is what permits him to use a trial and error strategy. His associations are more influential in his thinking, but he does not confuse them as often with causes. His dreams may be more upsetting now than at any other level. As in other areas, things are partly inside and partly outside himself, and in dreams these two realities become disturbingly mixed.

PERSONALITY OBJECTIVES FOR PRESCHOOL-AGED CHILDREN

Temperament

1. To deal with the realities of the environment within the limits of individual temperament.

Creativity/Expressiveness

1. To be able to use imagination in play.
2. To desire to produce something through his activity.
3. To engage in social play activities.
4. To engage in constructive play.

Self-Concept

1. To see himself as a person with genuine self-consciousness.
2. To recognize certain characteristics or actions as applying to him.
3. To make positive references (i.e., spontaneous comments) to what he can do.
4. To think of himself as being able to perform level-appropriate developmental tasks.

Fantasy

1. To express his concepts, concerns, fears, and questions through play activities.

2. To talk to himself about what is happening in his play.

3. To imagine a story from a series of pictures.

4. To begin to realize that fact and fantasy are different.

5. To engage in "pretend" play in which children assume roles.

6. To tell original, fanciful stories.

Emotional Reactions and Concerns

1. To express emotion at developmentally appropriate levels.

2. To use motor activity for the expression and release of tension.

3. To become increasingly verbal in the expression of feelings.

4. To become increasingly able to show concern for others.

Ego Development

1. To understand the concept of possession or ownership.

2. To recognize the wills of adults as being separate from his own will.

3. To accept change with relative ease.

4. To abide by rules when others are there to enforce them.

5. To relate to others in a reciprocal manner.

WHAT THE TEACHER DOES

Temperament.   You should respect each child's temperament, but it is not appropriate for you to try to change it. It is true that the temperament of some children makes it easier to work with them in the classroom than other children. Your role is to observe the child's behavior (i.e., his activity level, his response to stimulation, his approach to new activities, his distractability, and his ability to adjust) and to structure the program so that he can deal as effectively as possible with his environment. Your responsibility is to make adjustments in the program and in the techniques that are used in working with the children in order to get the best response from them.

Some children become overstimulated when they play actively with groups of children for a long period of time. When they play for too long, these children become difficult to control. If a quiet or individual activity is planned for those who become easily over-stimulated, this behavior can often be prevented. Quiet corners in the room where children can work alone or retreat with a book may be attractive to some. Keeping groups small helps to prevent over-stimulation. The noise level of too many children in one room can be an overstimulating factor.

Some children can sit quietly and listen to a story or look at a book; some cannot. Some children race madly around the playground, and others seem hardly ever to run or really engage in active play. It is reasonably easy to provide outdoor activity if adequate space is available, but you may need to initiate active play for children who stand and shake when the weather is cold or can never seem to get involved in active play. You can help restless children by selecting short stories and interspersing the quiet listening activity with rhythms that give the children an opportunity to be active or with participation in actions accompanying a story. One way to avoid a problem with restless children is to permit some of them to leave the story or group activity when they are tired. Since there should be more than one adult with each group of preschool children, it is unnecessary for all children to do the same thing at the same time or for the same length of time. Children who are tired of listening to a story can quietly leave the group and move to some other nondisturbing activity. Some children can go to the playground earlier than others. Some children can listen to a long story which is read by an assistant teacher while more active children can build with blocks or take a pretend trip to the beach. Since children of this level normally engage in much active play if the opportunities are provided, problems more often arise when they are expected to be quiet and still than when they are expected to be active.

Some children are distracted from an activity by the slightest interruption while some will work on one activity during the whole work period with all kinds of things going on around them. Some children are less distracted if you sit with them and respond to their conversation while they are working with clay or other table activities or if you stay near them and give a little help when a difficulty is encountered in whatever they are doing. You should capitalize on the child's special interests and give him encouragement in the form of comments or assistance over difficult spots. A child's success is vital to lessening his distractibility.

Children who are slow to approach new activities need time to warm up to a new situation. Some children will watch other children engage in rhythms for several weeks or longer before they show any response. Other children will stand back and wait until everyone else has petted the kitten before showing any interest. This behavior is offset by other children who crowd in to be the first at everything. Although children should be encouraged to participate, no one needs to be pushed to do things before he is ready. More eager and impulsive children can be encouraged to wait for a turn but only as long as it is feasible. You should plan to prevent too much crowding in one spot because these children become disruptive if they are expected to wait very long. Waiting is very difficult for most preschoolers and usually should be avoided if possible.

Some children adjust to school with ease and adjust to changes in the schedule or program with equal ease. Other children may need their mothers to stay with them for several days or even weeks. Some will need shorter days at the beginning of the year because they become too tired. There are disturbances of eating, sleeping, and toileting habits associated with adjustment to school which need matter-of-fact treatment until the child feels at ease. A child may need to bring an old cuddly blanket or stuffed toy to school until he has forgotten about it.

The individual characteristics of all children need your attention. The preceding suggestions do not include all of the situations in which differences need to be considered. Only examples are given. On the one hand, differences need to be encouraged, but a certain amount of conformity is necessary for life in society. In the beginning, you should make considerable concession to the child's behavior. Gradually, you can help to modify some of his behavior so that it is more within the realm of what society expects.

Creativity/Expressiveness.   You can do a great deal to encourage or discourage creativity and expressiveness by the kind of play you encourage and the kind of guidance you give. Younger preschoolers need an opportunity and the encouragement to enjoy the process of manipulating many materials, pulling and tugging blocks around, putting the doll to bed, feeding it, and pushing it in the carriage. This involvement with the process without the pressure to make anything provides the background for imaginative and creative play.

The richness of the child's cognitive and social experience is a positive factor in leading toward the creative use of ideas, but the kinds of classroom materials and the suggestions that you give to the children can make a difference in the creativity with which they use their ideas. Children will be more creative in the housekeeping area if you change some of the materials from time to time to correspond to the children's changing interests. For example, props such as a nurse's kit, a doll's suitcase, some empty food cartons, a doll's high chair, an ironing board, or dress-up clothes can add new interest. Stories, filmstrips, trips, or your suggestions can provide new ideas for the children.

In the woodworking area, you can provide pieces of wood in various shapes, odds and ends of washers, screws, bottle caps, and letters or numerals to be nailed on boards to suggest different ideas to the children. In the block area, accessory toys such as people, animals, and transportation toys suggest ways that the blocks can be used.

If you provide objects to be copied or directions to be followed, the use of art materials becomes stereotyped and children begin to try to please you. It is better for you to emphasize the different ways that materials can be used and the different effects that can be accomplished. Above all, it is important for you to show appreciation for the product that the child has created that is uniquely his. You can help to increase children's interest for art media such as clay, paste, or finger paint if you either sit at a table with the children or stay nearby while they are working. You can further help them if you work with some of the clay by squeezing it out and rolling pieces like the children do. Avoid making animals or other forms that the children recognize as being something they cannot do; this leads to requests for you to make them one. Also avoid projects where you have to do most of the work or give the children a lot of directions for how to make something, as this encourages children to rely on you for help and ideas about what to do. Children do pick up ideas from other children and this seems to be a friendly way of sharing. Supply a wide variety of artistic media over a period of weeks and keep the materials in the proper condition because children are easily discouraged by hard clay, dried-up paste, and muddy colored paint.

Encourage children to talk and use language in a variety of ways. This is discussed at length in Chapter Five so further ideas will not be given here except to point out that language is one of the most important means of creative expression.

Rhythms and movement offer very good opportunities for creative expression. The sheer enjoyment of movement gives the child a feeling of control, and he likes to experiment and see what he can do with his body. Suggest that children try to move to music in different ways, that they do tricks with their bodies, or that they show how they think a flower grows. It often helps if you move freely with the children but avoid making your movement something that the children copy.

Encouraging creativity is related to the way that you plan your entire program. You will not do very much to encourage creative expression if you reserve your encouragement for certain parts of the day. Encourage decision making and problem solving in many different situations. Plan your daily schedule so it will be flexible enough to adjust to the use of children's ideas. Listen to the children and facilitate the implementation of their ideas. Children need your help to feel good about the thoughts and products they produce not because it looks like something or looks like a preconceived idea but because it represents their work.

Self-Concept.   One of the most important contributions that the preschool program can make to the child's development is to help him regard himself as a worthwhile person who is deserving of self-respect and the respect of other people. This means that the personality and abilities of the child must be treated with respect despite the possibility that his behavior may be disturbing or destructive and his appearance may be unattractive.

With the youngest preschoolers, you can use teaching techniques which help the children to see themselves as persons. Opportunities for the child to see himself and other children in a mirror, to sing songs and rhymes which incorporate his name, and to engage in conversation in which parts of his body are named are important in helping the child gain a consciousness of himself as a person. Later he will like to see photographs of his activities at school, he will become interested in his maleness or femaleness, and he will respond to opportunities to talk about himself. These activities could all be described as ways of helping the child to feel important.

Success is essential to the development of a positive self-concept. If the child is to feel successful, he must be successful. You must plan activities at which he can be successful most of the time. Some activities should challenge him to give his best efforts. You can help him feel success by pointing out what he has been able to do and by encouraging him to attempt activities within his abilities.

It is essential for a child to feel that people like him. As the teacher, you are the most important person next to his family in helping him to feel liked. Some children are very personable and receive a favorable response from children and adults. Others may not be so fortunate. Their behavior may not be acceptable to adults or children, and they may be physically unattractive or dirty. Your greatest problem may be in actually liking some children. If it is, for whatever reason, you need to be aware of this. You may not be able to like every child, but you can try. Even knowing you do not like someone may help you find others who do like him and may help in controlling your reaction to him. Every child does not have to be liked by everyone but he has to be liked by enough people so that he can acquire a basic feeling of what it means to be liked, to have a friend to do something with, and to have someone with whom to share a secret or a favorite toy. Having two adults in the classroom is often an asset since a child who is having difficulty relating to one adult may get a different response from the second adult.

Usually, if the cognitive aspects of your program are appropriate for the children, those who come to school with a positive self-concept will feel good about themselves and their performances at school if the adults are reasonably adequate in their relationships with the children. Children who come to school feeling inadequate, unaccepted, or hostile are the ones who will need extra success experiences, special attention when you plan activities that are related to their interests, and special recognition for slight progress. Frequently, these are the children who seem to alienate the other children and to irritate the teacher, yet they have the greatest need for acceptance and recognition. You must find a way to give recognition for the behavior that you wish to promote. Behavior which is indicative of self-concept may change slowly so do not expect immediate results. Other times, it changes more rapidly.

Fantasy. You can encourage children to engage in fanciful experiences by providing the setting and the opportunity for them to use them freely. With younger preschoolers, the setting for housekeeping and other dramatic play is especially important. Usually, your role should be that of an observer and learner rather than that of an intervener except when relationship problems threaten to disrupt the situation. Fantasy play sometimes involves themes of violence and destruction which have to be guided cautiously, balancing the importance of expression by some children against the potential danger to other children and the disruption of the rest of the class. Some loud and active fantasy play which can be permitted on the playground will have to be controlled in the classroom. For example, gangster play or war play usually cannot be allowed in the classroom, but this play may be permitted outdoors where there is more space for running and where yelling and screaming do not matter; this play should be closely supervised so that it remains safe and does not involve unwilling participants.

Books, stories, and pictures play an important role in the child's fantasy life at school. Children like to talk about the events in a story; they like to talk about pictures in books and other pictures that the teacher brings in. You can use a variety of pictures in this way from those which are quite simple involving familiar content to those which are quite abstract or represent highly complex situations. Gradually, as children begin to tell complex, imaginary stories about pictures, their stories can be recorded. Children can later create and illustrate their own stories without the use of pictures to suggest the content. Creative dramatics also provides a way for older preschoolers to act out stories in detail.

Sometimes with older preschoolers it is a good idea to ask at the end of a story which has been read to children, Could this story really happen? In the discussion which follows, you can help the children discuss what is real and what is fanciful. Many preschool children have difficulty making this distinction, but some children who seem to believe their own tall tales may find the distinction especially difficult. You want to preserve the child's ability to be imaginative but, at the same time, to help him realize that he is being imaginative and not telling something which actually did or could happen.

Emotional Reactions and Concerns.   The preschoolder's expressions of anger and temper frequently present problems for the teacher. Children who have tantrums at home usually have a few when they first come to school. You will sometimes be surprised at the intensity of emotional expression that results from a relatively simple situation. While the situation triggers the tantrum, it is unlikely that the cause is quite so simple. At the time that you deal with the tantrum, you must also think of ways to deal with the real problem. Try, if possible, to avoid situations which cause violent outbursts. If you cannot avoid the issue and the child reacts with a tantrum, one thing should be quite clear—the situation does not change because of the child's intense reaction to it. If a valid judgment on your part led to the tantrum, it is still a valid judgment. The tantrum does not change it. After he stops the kicking and screaming, you can talk with him about your decision but give as little attention to the actual temper outburst as possible. Do not ignore the fact that an unusually intense expression has been caused. In response to this outburst, you can examine your program to see where the child feels this great sense of frustration and possibly make some changes in your expectations for the children. Make certain that there is ample opportunity for large motor activity and that this particular child engages in it. Activities such as water play, carpentry, working with clay, throwing balls, bean bags and other objects, punching a punching bag, and using finger paint are especially helpful in the expression of emotion and the release of tensions if the children are allowed to use the materials freely within the realm of reason and safety.

The child who expresses anger as an attack on another child, or perhaps an adult, also presents a difficult problem. You must protect the other children as a matter of safety, and you must also restrict the behavior because of the difficulties that the child will have if the other children are afraid of him. A child who attacks others has to be watched constantly and the preventive approach of engaging him in activities that relieve frustration and tension is one positive approach. Having to share toys, sitting still for more than a few minutes, waiting, and having to be quiet are all especially difficult tasks for this kind of child, and they should be avoided as long as he cannot accept less demanding limitations. Gradually, you can help the child to verbalize his anger or to verbally express what he wants or how he feels. Model behavior that you want the child to learn. For example, you might say to him, "Tell Jim you were using the blocks," "Tell Sam it hurts when he hits you," "Ask Juan for the truck when he has finished with it," or "I can't let you hit Sarah because you might hurt her."

Children can deal with pain much more easily if you face up to the fact of painfulness than if you deny it. You can use statements such as "It will hurt a little when we put the medicine on, but it will make your finger feel better," or "When the doctor gives you the shot, it will hurt but it will keep you from getting sick." It is much better for the child to cry a little and be soothed for it rather than to tell him it will not hurt only to have him discover that it does. In case something will hurt, you should prepare the child for it and then help him handle his reaction. This is an honest approach and inspires trust on the child's part whereas denying it inspires distrust and denial.

The handling of fear in the classroom is usually less of a problem to the teacher than the handling of anger and pain. Perhaps this is because the child who has many mild fears is helped by the presence of other children who are not afraid of the same things. Allow children who are afraid to watch from a distance, to try an activity with your assistance, or to proceed on their own with your reassurance; however, they should not be forced into a situation where they are afraid. Sometimes it is helpful if a child can be given a technique for handling a situation. Remember that children have to be taught caution and that separating fear from caution is difficult for them.

Usually, the approach to dealing with emotional reactions is to handle them as they arise; however, there are situations which give rise to emotional reactions which are known ahead of time and which can be planned for. For example, a child can be helped to plan for a trip to the hospital that is known in advance or to prepare for the arrival of a new baby in the family. There are some books which deal with events such as going to the dentist or the hospital. There are also books which deal with a variety of feelings. You can read these books to the children and follow with a discussion of the ways that they feel.

As a teacher, you are very much involved in the expression of emotion and in teaching ways to express it. In particular, you model acceptable expressions of emotion which show concern for the feelings of children and help them show concern for the feelings of other children. You accept and work with the feelings although the behavioral expression may not be acceptable. Your behavior in situations involving emotional expression is very important in establishing the atmosphere of the classroom. Children differ widely in their emotional reactivity, and the goal is to help them cope with situations in ways which will lead to their future well-being. You should expect that the children will learn to cope in different ways.

Ego Development.   The extent to which the child's ego development proceeds smoothly is dependent upon how well the many needs of the child are being met in the many situations which make up his experience. The school is just one of the many situations that affects ego development. For the most part, objectives given here have already been discussed in previous sections of this chapter.

Appropriate guidance seems to lie in the area of respect for the individual and the unique way that he is developing and responding to his environment. This respect allows him to be himself, doing things in his own way, and become an individual in his own right. There is much room for this kind of individuality within the limits imposed by society.

part three

Planning for Individual Children

The approach which we have taken has centered on the individual child. By looking at objectives separately, however, we run the risk of working with behaviors in isolation instead of working with the whole child. In the following chapter, we consider how to plan for the total child instead of for individual behaviors.

chapter 7

Seeing Objectives
in Terms of
the Total Child

Importance of Considering the Whole Child

Research on the development of young children has provided few solid leads as to how the different areas of development relate to each other. This is an unfortunate gap in our knowledge, but we cannot be content to wait for research to provide the answers. The children with whom we work continue to develop and require our guidance; they cannot wait for research to unlock these secrets of how the parts of development make up a complete child. Professionals who work with young children cannot know the answers, but they can think through what is happening within each child. It is possible, by carefully studying each child with whom we work and then by reflecting on all of the information which we obtain, to reach some reasonable conclusions that will guide our planning.

Consider what may happen if we do not consider the whole child. Suppose a child is lagging in motor development because he is slow to accept new experiences and therefore tries fewer new things. His cognitive development may be affected by this tendency as well, since rather than expressing an average amount of curiosity he will be overly cautious. Imagine that we attempt to work with him on some objectives in motor development or cognitive development while ignoring how he experiences the world and in turn how he relates to the physical environment. The child and we will be frustrated by the experience. It makes more sense to try to understand the child's overall approach to things and then to plan for his learning in an informed manner.

How to Consider the Whole Child

The case study approach allows us to consider the whole child (see Chapter 8). We gather all available information on the child. If we find gaps in this information, we either observe the child, test him, or seek help from a qualified person who can gather the needed information rapidly. Then we organize the information so that we can make brief summary statements about each area of development. Review and revise the summary statements to make sure that they accurately reflect the available information. The final step is to organize these statements into an overall summary. The Teacher's Observational Guide (Appendix B) will not do this job, but it will 1) serve as a useful checklist of how thorough you have been in gathering the needed information and 2) group the areas of development in a manner that should make the search for a better understanding easier.

Understanding how the parts of development form the whole is a matter of intuition. But it is not blind intuition; it is intuition which has been influenced by all the information that you have carefully assembled. Your intuition is also influenced by your understanding which is based on all your prior experience with individual children. If you are not experienced, you will appreciate the insights of a more experienced early childhood colleague.

When you think that you understand the child, discuss your impressions with the people who know him best—his parents. If your interpretations make sense to them and correspond to their understanding, this consensus is as near to certainty as you can hope to come. Of course, this is not a one-time effort, even though the discussion here tends to create that impression. Understanding any child is a continuous effort of updating. Some themes will, however, continue to reappear in the child's life, thus providing a continuity in the face of the changes which are forever appearing.

SELECTING PRIORITY OBJECTIVES TO ACHIEVE BALANCE

After you finish updating your understanding of the child, select a priority objective for him. Suppose you recognize that a child in your program is delayed in one or two areas because of a lag in another area. If this lag can be overcome, then the child will be able to catch up in the other areas. An objective in the area of the lag would be a priority objective.

You might select another priority objective for a quite different reason. Your case study of a particular child might reveal that he has all of the prerequisite competencies for certain experiences. He just has not put these competencies together to form certain new ones because he has not had the needed experiences. In this case, your priority would be in response to his readiness.

A third example will show another circumstance which may help you to set priorities. Suppose that you have discussed the child's progress with his parents and have learned that they could provide some new opportunities for him. Maybe they have not done so because they have sensed that he is not ready yet. Perhaps his mother could take him to play with another child but does not do so because of certain problems the two children have of getting along together. The preschool might help in this instance by setting priority objectives that would make this child ready to take part in this outside experience. This provides an excellent opportunity to work with the parents at meeting the child's developmental needs. You will probably think of other circumstances that lead to setting priorities. This list is not exhaustive.

In the process of setting priorities, take care to maintain balance. There is a particular danger in emphasizing objectives in areas of lagging development because the child may not be provided with opportunities in those areas where he is progressing. You can be sure that you are about to lose balance if the majority of your effort is directed to a single area of the child's development. Each child needs to develop in all areas and should have the opportunity and stimulation to do so. You should seek to identify priority objectives in the cognitive, the social and emotional, and the perceptual and motor areas.

RECOGNITION OF CHANGING PRIORITIES

The child's development continues to progress. What he did a month ago may no longer provide him challenge or hold his interest. Your case study of the child must be updated frequently. At times, the organization of the child's interests and the developmental challenges to which he reacts with motivation will change enough to require much rethinking of his program. You will be in a position to change your priorities when the child changes his priorities if you stay in touch with his development by gathering information on what he is presently doing. Changes will be required by circumstances, too. A visitor in his home, a different kind of involvement of his parent or sibling in his life, a new favorite toy become occasions for at least temporary shifts of priority. Sometimes circumstances may call for longer shifts of priority. The child's rate of development may also have an effect on priorities.

Patterns of Development in Young Children

This section examines some ways in which children develop patterns of behavior. Some children will clearly show different patterns. Knowing about these patterns can be helpful in planning for the whole child. A child's pattern of development may become apparent while you are doing a case study. Once it has been recognized, this will deserve careful reexamination over a fairly long period of the child's life. It is possible for us to examine only a few of the possible patterns of individual development. Those that we consider are patterns of temperament, interest and motivation, motor preference, and cognitive or learning style.

TEMPERAMENT PATTERNS IN YOUNG CHILDREN

Children differ in the overall pace or rate of their activity and in their reactions to novel stimulus situations, attention, and emotional reactions. These are some aspects of temperament. We recognize that temperament underlies the child's behavior when a general style becomes apparent across a wide variety of circumstances.

Some children are very easy to teach. They are not particularly excitable, their attention is good, they seem particularly eager to please or to fit in, and they easily take new happenings in stride. Such children are called highly adaptable. Another child from the same family and at the same age level may be irritable, very easily excited, contrary, and difficult to deal with in new situations. Another child may be overly shy, withdrawing and reluctant in the face of anything new, and able to adjust to new demands or routines only after long and patient emphasis. Such very different temperament styles have numerous implications for the child's learning, needs for adult help and guidance, and adjustment.

Other temperament related differences may be less extensive than these. Children may be active in many situations or very lethargic or slow moving. Some children become very excited when they are stimulated, even when they are well rested and other conditions are favorable to calmness. Others appear to remain calm and unperturbed in many arousing situations. One child will stop whatever he is doing when an opportunity arises to do something else while another child can hardly be pried away from his activities, even to do something which you know he enjoys doing. Some children are buoyantly cheerful even when conditions lead you to expect the worst; others seem always on the verge of frustration and negative emotional reactions. Such differences are not simply traceable to something that children have learned. They represent fundamental, individual variations of temperament in many instances.

INTEREST-MOTIVATION

Individual differences in this area are most often either reflections of the child's developmental stage or of the ways he has learned to behave. Thus, unlike the case with temperament, we expect the child to change gradually in these respects.

Some children are very much attracted to the physical environment. They are challenged by the opportunity to touch, examine, manipulate, and generally have an effect upon objects in the environment. For many children, this represents a phase through which they pass, but for others it is an enduring characteristic. Other children are more interested in the people around them than they are in things. They prefer the opportunity to get attention or to interact with persons over whatever else they have been doing. Children who tend strongly in either of these directions will learn more easily from sources of the preferred type and will have difficulty adapting to the other type.

We may suspect that the child who is more interested in things than people has not found people to be very rewarding or interesting. It may be beneficial to such a child to form a close attachment to an adult who is willing to be very attentive to what the child is doing. On the other hand, the child who is predominantly interested in people and who derives little pleasure from objects in the physical environment may not have experienced much success or pleasure in the physical environment. This may be the result of a lack of opportunity to manipulate materials at an early age, some perceptual or motor difficulty, or a lack of intellectual drive. Sometimes, such a child may be interested in manipulating simple materials, which he would not normally have available at his advanced age level.

Another source of individual differences is a preference for the company of peers or adults. For preschoolers, adults continue to be a primary focus of interest, but over the years of early childhood, interest in peer contact typically increases. Apparently, early preferences for peer contact are fostered by early opportunities for peer contact in an environment which contains enough play materials to prevent competition among the children. Since an over-dependence on adults is detrimental to the child's social progress and to school readiness, it is generally considered desirable to foster the child's interest in peers.

VARIATIONS IN MOTOR PREFERENCE

Everyone who works with young children eventually becomes aware of their preferences for one hand over another. Differences in dominance, handedness, or laterality have received considerable and often excessive emphasis. An often more useful distinction can be made regarding the child's preference for gross motor versus fine motor activities. As in the case of the preceding section, this is often very much a matter of developmental phases. The relative emphasis will shift as the child grows older. Whether the child's preference is developmental or whether it proves to be more enduring, the preference influences what the child attempts to do.

The child who prefers fine motor activities may spend a considerable amount of time in manipulative activities such as stacking, arranging, building, drawing, painting, and copying. These activities tend to promote the integration of hand-eye coordination. Children who prefer such activities may, therefore, be more advanced in their tactile and visual perceptions. A child's preference for gross motor activity is expressed by his vigorous movement, running about, climbing, tussling, swinging, and riding a variety of toy vehicles. A great amount of this activity produces increased balance, coordination, gross motor competency, and often successful efforts to be physically competitive. Some children show a considerable balance between gross and fine motor activities. These children will eventually be competent and versatile in sports activities, since many active sports require a combination of gross and fine motor skills.

Sometimes you will suspect that a child avoids either fine or gross motor activities in order to avoid frustration or failure. You will be alerted to this possibility if the child appears to be particularly awkward and/or easily frustrated when he attempts to do things which require him to use his nonpreferred motor system. Whenever your observations suggest this, an expert opinion is desirable. Some remedial work may be carried out by an occupational or a physical therapist to give the child greater competency in his area of motor weaknesses.

VARIATIONS IN COGNITIVE STYLE

This is an area of child behavior which has been studied only in recent years. We may expect, from what has already been learned about the importance of cognitive style, that even more attention will be given in the future to these sources of individual differences.

One aspect of cognitive style is called *conceptual tempo.* This refers to the fact that some children tend to be more reflective while others are more impulsive in solving problems. For example, the reflective child tends to spend more time looking at and studying a set of illustrated answer choices before picking the one he believes to be correct. If the problem requires him to match a choice to a particular standard, he carefully compares the various answer choices to the standard. All of this checking takes time, so he answers slowly but is likely to be correct. The impulsive child spends little time in making an answer choice and is likely to make many mistakes on problems which require him to select a best answer. He does not seem to reflect upon the alternatives. Most children become increasingly reflective toward the close of the preschool years, but some children basically continue to be impulsive even after they have entered school.

Some children form global impressions while others pay a great deal of attention to detail. These children are sometimes referred to, respectively, as *global* and *analytic.* The child with a global style will form a general impression of something that he has experienced, but this may not accurately reflect the details. If he is questioned afterwards, he will be unable to recall many details. The child of an analytic style does not emphasize the overall impression. When he tells a story, for example, he may not come to the point or give the essentials. Instead, he relates in fine detail what happened first, next, next, and next, until people may tire of listening to him.

Several other cognitive styles have been identified and are actively being investigated, but they are too numerous to consider in detail here. The reader who wants to pursue this topic further will find frequent references to cognitive style studies in the journal *Child Development Abstracts and Bibliography.* In any event, the two sets of contrasting styles which were discussed should prove useful to your understanding of some young children and how they approach learning.

part four

Evaluation

Early childhood programs would not be complete without a plan for evaluating children's growth and progress. This final section of the book discusses several approaches to evaluating children's progress. Various methods, which may be utilized in the evaluation process, are described along with examples of their use. Since communicating and reporting to parents are vital components of any program, suggestions are also provided for implementing these processes.

chapter 8

Evaluating and Reporting Progress

Observing Children's Progress

Too often, teachers make observations of children only when they are misbehavior problems. You should observe the behavior of all the children under your supervision if you are to fully plan for their total progress through the year.

Much of your observation will occur spontaneously. For example, as you move about the classroom, you may hear children using new words which you have not heard them use before. You will hear children give explanations for their activities or for the materials with which they are working that you have never heard them give before. You will see a child climb to a new height on the climbing apparatus or see a child walk a balance beam for the first time. You will hear a child offer to share for the first time or see a child's first endeavor toward cooperative play. Many, many events occur for the first time in the preschool classroom.

There will be times when you will plan to watch a particular child participating in some particular activity. You may need information about what materials would be more appropriate for the child to use. You may need information to indicate how the child plays with other children. You may be considering the special needs of the child and need observations to decide if special needs actually exist or to what extent they require special attention.

When you are first developing skills of observation, it helps to focus on a specific developmental characteristic. For example, it is easy to define certain gross motor abilities such as running, skipping, or jumping. To practice your observation skills, you should identify a specific skill to watch for, particularly if you are observing spontaneous behaviors. With specific skills such as classification, cutting, copying, or climbing, you can set up activities which will allow you to focus on one skill area at a time.

You will also be observing the progress of the child. What happens after that first time is just as important to your understanding of the child as the first event. You will be watching to see if the child continues the new behavior. For example, the child's first attempts at sharing, hopefully, will be followed by more sharing episodes. Since these events will occur spontaneously, you must be alert to their occurrence.

RECORDING CHILDREN'S PROGRESS

Regardless of your expertise as an observer of children's behavior, you will want to set up some kind of a system for recording your observations. Keeping good records on children's progress is a time-consuming task for the teacher. Thus, a good system of record keeping is a necessity.

There are four basic methods for recording children's progress. These four, with some variations, are anecdotal records; checklists; case studies; and scales, tests, and inventories.

Anecdotal Records. Anecdotal records consist of anecdotes or incidents which are recorded either as they happen or as soon after they happen as possible. These are incidents which give you some insight into the child's behavior and provide a basis for planning his program.

Anecdotal records provide more details as to the child's behavior than a checklist does. They will include specific actions and language used by the child. To cite an example, consider recording a child's ability to walk a balance beam. If he successfully crosses the balance beam, you could check him off on the checklist and be done with it. If he should be a child who was still insecure, had to try several times before actually managing to cross the balance beam, and then was very wobbly as he crossed it, you would lose this information on a checklist. On an anecdotal record, however, you could record your notes of the child's progress, as follows:

> James walked to the balance beam hesitantly. He tried three times before he could balance himself on it. As he tried to walk it the first time, he kept putting his left foot down to the floor to catch himself. When he was halfway across, he slipped off on both feet. He came back to the end and started again. This time he also placed his left foot on the floor to balance himself. He walked to the other end and stepped off. Then he started back and walked the entire length of the beam without touching either foot to the floor. He was very wobbly but did not slip. He had a big smile on his face when he finished.

This record indicates that James needs more practice and that he has been successful but may not be ready to be placed entirely on his own yet. Even though you might remember this incident in detail and know even with just a checklist that James needs more help, you will have many such incidents to remember, and some will slip from your memory.

The value of anecdotal records will become apparent to you as you use them. You may decide that some activities can only be recorded through anecdotal records while others can be successfully handled through other forms of records.

Language which gives insight into children's understanding is useful in anecdotal records. How does a child explain his use of certain colors or materials? Why did he place the blue triangle with the red triangle instead of placing it with the blue square? Keeping records of the child's language signals will give you cues to his thinking and to the development which is taking place within him. Without these cues and records of them, you might not plan the appropriate experiences for him.

When you record anecdotes, try to report only what you see taking place. Avoid being overly descriptive. Too many adjectives often imply your interpretation of what you are seeing, particularly in terms of children's feelings. An interpretative statement may follow an incident, but it should not be part of the recorded anecdote.

Checklists.   Checklists serve several purposes. They are a simple and quick means of recording children's behavior. Repeated anecdotes of a given situation will sometimes lead to the development of a comprehensive checklist. For example, as a result of watching several children who are learning to walk the balance beam, you might devise a checklist such as:

☐   1.   Approaches balance beam with caution and cannot stand on it.

☐   2.   Can stand on balance beam for ____ seconds.

☐   3.   Attempts to walk balance beam but drops left/right foot to balance himself.

☐   4.   Can walk balance beam one way.

☐   5.   Can walk balance beam both ways.

☐   6.   Can walk balance beam backwards.

A variation of a checklist which includes some components of the anecdotal records provides space for comments beside each item.

You could use the preceding checklist on a form for an individual child. Another kind of checklist can be used for the whole class or for a group of children. This form would list a number of activities or concepts across the top with space for each child's name down the side. As each child completes an activity, his name is checked off or the date is entered. This is a simple way to keep records that require no explanation on abilities or activities.

Case Studies.   The case study consists of a detailed description of all phases of the child's life. Some components of a case study are usually a part of any good set of preschool records; for example, you probably already have health histories, family histories, interest inventories, etc. In contrast to the randomness of keeping anecdotal records, the records for a case study are carefully planned so that they include a total systematic view of the child's behavior.

You will probably use the case study for children who seem to have special needs or special learning problems. By making a complete careful observation of such children, you will be able to enlist help from other community and school resources to aid them. You will also find your records to be helpful if parents need to be convinced of their child's special needs.

Scales, Tests, and Inventories.   Another method of evaluation which you may use consists of scales, tests, and inventories. A variety of these instruments exists for use with preschool children.[2] The appropriateness of each instrument depends upon what you are assessing and how each instrument can add information to what you already know about the children.

Since these instruments focus upon the child at a given time, they may be inadequate for assessing his progress in the program. Match your evaluation instruments with your goals and developmental objectives for the children.

Some of these instruments can be administered by the classroom teacher, but many require special training and experience to administer. Unless you need these tests for special purposes, you will probably gain just as much useful information about the children from careful observations.

COMMUNICATING CHILDREN'S PROGRESS

You will need to indicate the children's progress to their parents and to other staff members. The records which you keep will be helpful as you prepare your report. You can also use them to support any interpretation that you must make regarding the child's behavior.

You can better communicate reports to parents through a conference. In a conference, you can avoid misunderstandings and misinterpretations which often result from written reports. You can answer the parents' questions and thoroughly discuss any aspect of the child's behavior which needs your and the parents' attention. Many parents do not know what to expect of their preschool child, and often they are expecting too much. You can help the parent better understand his child through your reporting process.

Many teachers use checklists and written comments to keep parents aware of what is happening at school. If the parent receives an occasional note from the teacher, he will understand not only his child's progress but also the school program. Often you will want to make a phone call to the parent to discuss school incidents, to explain something that has happened at school, or to inquire as to the child's behavior at home. Often, a child's change of behavior at

---

[2] See A. Butler et al., *Literature Search and Development of an Evaluation System in Early Childhood Education,* Report III, Part B, "Evaluation Instruments," ERIC # Ed 059783, 1971.

school can be readily explained by events at home. A phone call is the quickest way to ascertain this.

There should be some discussion of the children's progress among staff members. How this is accomplished will depend upon the size of your staff. Staff meetings can provide an opportunity for the teachers to discuss children's behavior and development. Program planning meetings should always include some discussion of individual needs and plans to meet those needs. It may work best to assign each child to a specific staff member for observational purposes. You may make weekly assignments to each teacher to observe specific behaviors and characteristics.

The total child can be viewed only through a composite of teacher-parent observations and discussion. For this reason, keep the channels of communication open with all persons who are involved with the children in your classroom. The more systematically you can deal with the information that you receive from them, the better you will be able to deal with the progress of each child.

appendix a

References Used in the Preparation of
Developmental Sequences of Behavior

Aaronson, M., and Schaefer, E. S. *"Preschool Preposition Test."* Mimeographed. 1968. Write May Aaronson, N. I. M. H., Bethesda, Md. 20014.

Ames, L. B.; Metraux, R. W.; Rodell, J. L.; and Walker, R. N. *Child Rorschach Responses; Developmental Trends from Two to Ten Years.* New York: Brunner/Mazel, 1974.

Bayley, N. *Manual for the Bayley Scales of Infant Development.* New York: Psychological Corp., 1969.

Beery, K. E., and Buktenica, N. A. *Developmental Test of Visual Motor Integration.* Chicago: Follett Publishing Co., 1967.

Butler, Annie L., Gotts, Edward E., Quisenberry, Nancy L., and Thompson, Robert P. *Literature Search and Development of an Evaluation System in Early Childhood Education.* ERIC #ED 059780–784, 1971.

The Bzoch-League *Receptive-Expressive Emergent Language Scale.* Gainesville, Florida: Computer Management Corp.

Carmichael, Leonard, ed. *Manual of Child Psychology.* 2d ed. New York: John Wiley & Sons, 1954.

Cohen, H., and Weil, G. R. *Tasks of Emotional Development.* Lexington, Mass.: Lexington Books, 1971.

Crabtree, M. *The Houston Test for Language Development.* Houston, Texas: M. Crabtree, 10133 Bassoon, 1958.

Doll, E. A. *PAR. Preschool Attainment Record.* Research Edition. Circle Pines, Minn.: American Guidance Service, 1966.

———. *Vineland Social Maturity Scale.* Circle Pines, Minn.: American Guidance Service, 1965.

Dunn, L. M. *Peabody Picture Vocabulary Test.* Circle Pines, Minn.: American Guidance Service, 1959.

Frankenburg, W. K.; Dodds, J. B.; and Fandel, A. W. *Denver Developmental Screening Test Manual.* Rev. ed. Mead Johnson Laboratories, 1970.

Gesell, A. *Gesell Developmental Schedules.* New York: Psychological Corp., 1949.

Hejna, R. J. *Developmental Articulation Test.* Madison, Wisconsin: College Printing and Typing Co., 1955.

Hoffman, M. L., and Hoffman, L. W., eds. *Review of Child Development Research,* vol. 1. New York: Russell Sage Foundation, 1964.

————. *Review of Child Development Research,* vol. 2. New York: Russell Sage Foundation, 1966.

Izard, C. *The Face of Emotion.* New York: Appleton-Century-Crofts, 1971.

Janis, I. L. et al. "Personality Development." In *Personality, Dynamics, Development, and Assessment.* New York: Harcourt Brace Jovanovich, 1969.

Kirk, S. A.; McCarthy, J. J.; and Kirk, W. D. *Illinois Test of Psycholinguistic Abilities.* Rev. ed. Urbana, Ill.: University of Illinois Press, 1968.

Luria, A. R. *The Role of Speech in the Regulation of Normal and Abnormal Behavior.* New York: Liveright, 1961.

Mecham, M. J. *Verbal Language Development Scale.* Circle Pines, Minn.: American Guidance Service, 1959.

Meier, J. *Screening and Assessment of Young Children at Developmental Risk.* Washington, D.C.: The President's Committee on Mental Retardation, 1973.

Mussen, P. H., ed. *Carmichael's Manual of Child Psychology.* 3d ed. 2 vols., New York: John Wiley & Sons, 1970.

Paraskevopoulos, J. K., and Kirk, S. A. *The Development and Psychometric Characteristics of the Revised Illinois Test of Psycholinguistic Abilities.* Urbana, Ill.: University of Illinois Press, 1969.

Piaget, J., and Inhelder, B. *The Psychology of the Child.* New York: Basic Books, 1969.

Smith, H. C. *Personality Development.* New York: McGraw-Hill Book Co., 1968.

Sprugel, C. C., and Goldberg, S. *Developmental Guidelines Compiled from Selected Sources.* Mimeographed.

Terman, L. M., and Merrill, M. A. *Stanford-Binet Intelligence Scale, Form L-M.* 3d revision. Boston: Houghton Mifflin Co., 1960.

Wechsler, D. *Wechsler Intelligence Scale for Children.* New York: Psychological Corp., 1949.

Wenar, C. *Personality Development from Infancy to Adulthood.* Boston: Houghton Mifflin Co., 1971.

Wepman, J. M. *Wepman Scale of Language Development.* Mimeographed.

Zimmerman, I. L.; Steiner, V. G.; and Evatt, R. L. *Preschool Language Scale.* Columbus, Ohio: Charles E. Merrill Publishing Co., 1969.

appendix b

Teacher Observational Guides

Child's Name _____ Date of 1st obs. _____ 2nd obs. _____ 3rd obs. _____ 4th obs. _____ 5th obs. _____

PERCEPTUAL AND MOTOR SKILLS

Behavior	Developmental Level					Brief Description	Objective	Contributing Activities
	1st obs.	2nd obs.	3rd obs.	4th obs.	5th obs.			
Gross Motor								
Fine Motor								
Speech								
Growth and Maturation								

Child's Name _____ Date of 1st obs. _____ 2nd obs. _____ 3rd obs. _____ 4th obs. _____ 5th obs. _____

COGNITIVE SKILLS

Behavior	Developmental Level					Brief Description	Objective	Contributing Activities
	1st obs.	2nd obs.	3rd obs.	4th obs.	5th obs.			
Attention								
Perception								
Memory								
Concepts Objects								
Classes								
Number								

Space							
Time							
Causality							
Nature							
Language							
Mediation							
Problem Solving and Logical Thought							

Child's Name _____ Date of 1st obs. _____ 2nd obs. _____ 3rd obs. _____ 4th obs. _____ 5th obs. _____

SOCIAL AND EMOTIONAL DEVELOPMENT

Behavior	Developmental Level					Brief Description	Objective	Contributing Activities
	1st obs.	2nd obs.	3rd obs.	4th obs.	5th obs.			
Social Relations								
Social Skills								
Behavioral Controls								
Other Areas of Socialization Aggression/ Assertiveness								
Sex typing								
Maturity/ Responsibility								

Positive Social Behavior	Humor	Motivation Extrinsic	Intrinsic	Personality Temperament	Creativity/ Expressiveness	Self-Concept	Fantasy	Emotional Reactions and Concerns	Ego Development

appendix c

Objectives from Chapters 4, 5, and 6

PERCEPTUAL AND MOTOR OBJECTIVES

Gross Motor

1. To engage in a variety of activities which require balance and total body control.
2. To engage in a variety of activities which require rhythmic movement.
3. To dress oneself with the exception of tying and difficult fasteners.
4. To climb large climbing equipment such as slides, jungle gyms, fire poles, abstract climbers, etc.
5. To ride and guide wheel toys such as tricycles and wagons.

Fine Motor

1. To develop the hand control which is essential for writing, drawing, and handling eating utensils.
2. To develop the eye-hand coordination which is essential for using construction toys and moderately difficult puzzles and form boards.
3. To control scissors when roughly cutting (i.e., when cutting approximately) along the outline of a simple figure or design which the child has drawn.
4. To acquire the coordination needed for lacing, paper folding, buttoning, or loose tying.

Speech

1. To produce speech which is understood by a stranger.
2. To correctly reproduce consonant sounds and blends (i.e., *M, N, H, W, P, J* as in junior, *CH, S, B, Z, TR, BL, F, G, K, T,* and diphthongs *OU, OI.* The child may have trouble with *K* and *G* when they appear in blends. *TH, NG,* and *Y* as in un*i*on may be present.)

Growth and Maturation (guides for teachers and parents rather than specific objectives)

1. To keep accurate information regarding the child's height, weight, and head circumference in order to show the pattern of growth.
2. To provide proper conditions for rest and activity.
3. To provide for good nutrition and eating habits.
4. To help parents understand the importance of proper maturation and growth.

COGNITIVE OBJECTIVES

Attention

1. To direct attention to one activity of interest even though other activities are possible.
2. To redirect attention from one object to another.
3. To voluntarily focus on an appropriate activity or piece of equipment when requested to do so by the teacher (not before level IV).

Perception

1. To recognize new objects.
2. To recognize characteristics which distinguish one animate or inanimate object from another.
3. To hear and understand separate sounds and sound combinations (i.e., words, phrases, sentences).
4. To recognize something after seeing only part of it.
5. To recognize familiar objects from pictures.

Memory

1. To repeat simple nursery rhymes, poems, and songs that are used regularly at school.
2. To remember important personal data such as address and parents' names.
3. To recall the main details of stories, recite numbers in order, and follow at least three directions.

Concepts

Objects

1. To give more complete descriptions of the qualities of objects.

2. To show a growing awareness of abstract ideas (e.g., sweet, older, prettier, easy).

Classes

1. To verbally classify things according to whether they are the same or different (e.g., they look alike or they do not look alike; they sound alike or they do not sound alike).

2. To group things which go together.

Number

1. To arrange, on the basis of verbal instruction, objects of varying lengths from small to large so that they match a visible model.

2. To arrange three objects of varying sizes in order from small to large.

3. To tell which of two objects is larger or smaller.

4. To tell which of two areas is larger or smaller.

5. To acquire a vocabulary of number related words.

6. To count accurately. (See individual levels for counting expectations.)

7. To know the ordinal positions of first, middle, and last.

8. To understand that something that is cut into halves leaves two pieces.

Space

1. To acquire a receptive vocabulary for spatial relationships (e.g., top, middle, corner).

2. To develop a concept of distance (e.g., far, near).

3. To indicate the relative positions of things to one's body (e.g., behind, in front of, inside, outside).

4. To extend the concept of relative position from oneself to other objects (e.g., next to the table).

Time

1. To relate the times of the day to activities that take place during the day.

2. To use the future tense, present perfect tense, and the past perfect tense in addition to the present and past tenses.

3. To recognize before, after, later.

Causality

1. To seek information about cause-effect relationships.

2. To experience himself as a cause of things that happen in his environment.

3. To experience outside objects and things as causes and effects and to eventually understand that only animate things cause effects.

Nature

1. To recognize major land features and weather phenomena that are within the realm of the child's experience.

Language

1. To understand and use active and question sentences and increasingly to understand negative sentences and use passive sentences.

2. To use sentences that consist of six to seven words.

3. To increase in his ability to use the language forms of the adults around him.

4. To have the language structure and vocabulary to tell original stories.

5. To become increasingly able to pantomime experiences that he has had plus the experiences that he has observed in others.

6. To show an interest in the meaning of new and abstract words.

Mediation

1. To be able to form associations between pictures and verbal descriptions, between objects and labels, between objects

and functions, and between past experiences and present observations.

Problem Solving and Logical Thought

1. To engage in problem-solving experiences.

SOCIAL AND EMOTIONAL OBJECTIVES

Social Relations

1. To be relatively more oriented to other people rather than oriented to just his own desires.
2. To prefer associations with children over adults. (Level V only)
3. To gradually progress from parallel to cooperative relationships with other children (with frequent quarreling.)
4. To ask for help when it is needed.
5. To verbally express a preference for particular friends.
6. To move freely and safely in a familiar neighborhood.
7. To develop cooperative relationships with peers.
8. To give and take with a sense of loyalty to particular people.
9. To match behavior to social expectations which relate to sex typing.
10. To establish friendly interactions with adults other than his parents.

Social Skills

1. To imitate the behavior of significant adults and peers.
2. To be able to label emotions for which labels have been supplied.
3. To use imitation in order to learn about the realities of the social world (e.g., to practice "going to work" or "making the supper").
4. To recognize the emotions of characters in cartoons and picture stories.

5. To recognize how someone feels from observing his facial expression, verbal label, tone of voice, and context.

6. To have a general grasp of how another person might feel in a particular situation.

7. To be aware of family and occupational roles.

8. To be aware of social differences such as age, sex, race, speech and appearance in ethnic groups, and socio-economic levels.

Behavioral Controls

1. To respond to redirection better than to punishment or direct attempts to stop undesirable behavior.

2. To increase his ability to respond to verbal controls.

3. To become increasingly able to use self-direction in controlling behavior.

4. To use language as a means of controlling his behavior.

5. To increase his ability to understand what is meant by "good" behavior. (See levels I through V.)

6. To respond positively to insistence on "good" behavior. (The child may react negatively to over-insistence on "good" behavior.)

7. To conform to demands when it is known they will be followed up.

8. To obey and conform in order to avoid punishment.

9. To obey and conform in order to maintain favorable relationships with adults.

10. To have a simple idea of how "good" behavior leads to personal satisfaction.

Socialization

Aggression/Assertiveness

1. To exhibit controlled forms of aggression.

2. To exhibit aggression verbally rather than physically.

3. To use more indirect forms rather than direct forms of aggression.

Sex Typing

1. To be better able to identify feminine sex-typed objects and masculine sex-typed objects.

2. To conform more to the standards that are expected by adults in regard to sex typing.

3. To increasingly imitate adults of the same sex.

4. To show a preference for sex-typed toys.

Maturity/Responsibility

1. To become increasingly able to care for himself at the toilet with fewer day and nighttime accidents.

2. To become increasingly helpful to adults, especially when actions can be imitated.

3. To dress and undress himself with increasing responsibility.

4. To become increasingly willing to feed himself and handle eating utensils.

5. To increasingly handle responsibility for himself (e.g., washing hands, brushing teeth, having money).

Positive Social Behaviors

1. To become increasingly able to interact with peers, to share information, to cooperate with activities, and to converse.

2. To grow in his ability to share and take turns.

3. To be increasingly able to settle quarrels and differences by himself.

4. To engage in more competitive situations.

Humor

1. To laugh at his own actions and those of adults.

2. To laugh at silly or absurd statements.

Motivation

Extrinsic

1. To be responsive to adult approval and punishment.

2. To be responsive to concrete reinforcers.

3. To be responsive to social reinforcement.

4. To imitate behavior which is modeled by the adult.

Intrinsic

1. To be interested in exploring the immediate environment.

2. To be interested in being like his parents.

3. To want to make things.

4. To become interested in something that is presented and explained to him.

5. To want to maintain smooth relationships with adults.

6. To show curiosity by touching, looking at things, or asking questions.

Personality

Temperament

1. To deal with the realities of the environment within the limits of individual temperament.

Creativity/Expressiveness

1. To be able to use imagination in play.

2. To desire to produce something through his activity.

3. To engage in social play activities.

4. To engage in constructive play.

Self-Concept

1. To see himself as a person with genuine self-consciousness.

2. To recognize certain characteristics or actions as applying to him.

3. To make positive references (i.e., spontaneous comments) to what he can do.

4. To think of himself as being able to perform level-appropriate developmental tasks.

Fantasy

1. To express his concepts, concerns, fears, and questions through play activities.

2. To talk to himself about what is happening in his play.

3. To imagine a story from a series of pictures.

4. To begin to realize that fact and fantasy are different.

5. To engage in "pretend" play in which children assume roles.

6. To tell original, fanciful stories.

Emotional Reactions and Concerns

1. To express emotion at developmentally appropriate levels.

2. To use motor activity for the expression and release of tension.

3. To become increasingly verbal in the expression of feelings.

4. To become increasingly able to show concern for others.

Ego Development

1. To understand the concept of possession or ownership.

2. To recognize the will of adults as being separate from his own will.

3. To accept change with relative ease.

4. To abide by rules when others are there to enforce them.

5. To relate to others in a reciprocal manner.

appendix d

Examples of Daily Objectives for Individuals or Small Groups

We prepared the following lists to provide guidance for the teacher in the preparation of daily individual or small group objectives. These objectives would probably appear in the teacher's daily lesson plan. They are only brief examples. Many more activities could be based on other aspects of development or on the equipment and supplies that are available in the classroom.

These objectives are derived from the developmental sequences of behavior in the area of perception (see Chapter 5). The process to be followed in developing these daily objectives is to observe the child and find where his behavior fits in the developmental sequence. Select behaviors at that level which the child has not attained and write objectives for him. If the child seems to be in transition between two levels, plan some objectives from the higher level. Plan experiences that encourage the child to engage in the desired behavior. Observe what the child can do and offer him the encouragement and assistance that he needs.

Objective	What the Teacher Does
Level I	
To identify fine details in familiar pictures.	Provides picture books with clearly defined pictures and asks questions about the pictures as he sits and looks at them with a child.
To identify himself and children that he knows in photographs.	Finds someone to make pictures of the children and makes them available for the children to look at and talk about.
To repeat a new word that an adult pronounces.	Plans an experience that introduces new words to the children. Uses the new word and encourages the child to repeat it.

Level II

To put simple puzzles together.	Provides simple puzzles and form boards. Encourages the children to work the puzzles and gives them help when they experience difficulty.
To recognize known objects from small replicas.	Provides toys such as small animals, cars, trucks, etc. Talks to the children about what they are as they play with them.

Level III

To identify animals and objects from pictures.	Plays a naming game with the child in which the child selects a named animal or object from a group of pictures.
To match pictures of objects.	Provides games such as lotto which require the child to match pictures. Helps children who need clues to be successful.

Level IV

To match objects by color.	Provides an opportunity for children to put objects (e.g. blocks, crayons, beads, etc.) of the same color together.
To stack objects in order of size.	Provides toys of graduated size such as blocks which can be stacked or cans or cups which can be put inside each other.
To match sounds made by different objects.	Provides objects such as boxes or bottles with beans or stones inside to rattle. Helps child identify the ones that sound alike.

Level V

To copy simple mosaic or block designs.	Provides a variety of designs with beads, blocks, or mosaic tiles which the child can copy.

To recognize a penny, nickel, and dime.

Continues to provide challenging puzzles.

Plans experiences where children need to use coins to make simple purchases. Helps count the money and explains the names of the coins.

index